THE
HIRING TREE

THE HIRING TREE

LAWS OF APPLICANT ATTRACTION

STEVEN J. SMITH

SHRM-CP, PHR

The Hiring Tree: Laws of Applicant Attraction
Copyright © 2023 by Steven J Smith

Published in the United States by
The Hiring Tree, LLC,
thehiringtreebook.com

Cover Design: Miladinka Milic • milagraphicartist.com
Interior Book Design: Francine Platt • Eden Graphics, Inc.

First Edition, 2023

ISBN 979-8-9874370-0-1

*I want to dedicate this book to
Alicia and Mandee, whose friendship
provided the right environment to
develop the analogy for the Hiring Tree.*

TABLE OF CONTENTS

PROLOGUE

A DEAR FRIEND OF MINE told me that every good analogy begins with a story, which is good news, because there is definitely a unique story that led to the idea behind the "Hiring Tree" model described in this book. The first epiphany happened in the fall of 2014 when my family moved from Alabama to Utah. While it was not one single moment that led to the analogy, a lot of moments came together to build the concept of the Hiring Tree from the roots up. These experiences occurred in a very special place called Santaquin, Utah.

When I arrived in Salt Lake City and then drove south on I-15 for about two hours, I was awestruck by some of the most magnificent mountains that exist in the United States. In fact, they were so close to my vehicle, that it almost felt like I could touch them if I were to stretch out my arms far enough.

During the fall, these mountains are often blanketed with snow. I watched the scene unfold upon passing the city of Spanish Fork, at which point I veered west and came upon an even more alluring landscape, dotted with trees in the most gracefully placed rows. I quickly began to understand why Katherine Lee Bates described a similar scene in a popular patriotic song when she penned "Oh Beautiful! … For purple mountain majesties, Above the fruited plain!"

Sure enough, the fruited plains I was observing were placed

perfectly along the foothills of the mountains, along what locals call the "Wasatch Front." Exiting the freeway at Main Street for Santaquin, there were several neighborhoods that I had to maneuver through in a mouse-like maze before the road finally led me to a set of railroad tracks. The train's horn was blaring as it whizzed past me, heading to an unknown destination. Once safety resumed, I crossed the tracks and found what I was seeking, nestled near an array of grapevines along a hidden fence. Orchards of cherries, heavenly white nectarines, peaches and a variety of apples also dotted the landscape. I had come to my journey's end and found myself looking at a peaceful orchard known as Pyne Farms.

Farmer Pyne could be seen in a red-and-black-checkered flannel shirt, jeans, and some mountain-man boots designed to withstand the terrain he confronted each day. He waved his sun-darkened arm in an excited gesture to welcome me as he bumped up and down in an ancient-looking tractor that was chugging along the dirt road toward me.

I parked underneath an enormous tree that was much older than I was. To my right was a newly built and spacious building with a lift-gate garage door big enough to fit the very tractor Farmer Pyne was driving. I learned later that this building was a giant cooler, designed to hold the fruits of his labors, as picking season had already begun.

Once the humming of the engine died down upon his arrival, he hopped down and gave me a big hug. It had been several years since I had seen my friend Kent, though back then, he was not a farmer at all. In fact, his father had run the farm for years, inheriting it from his father, who had also inherited it from his father. As the new fourth-generation owner, it was now Kent's turn to run the farm with all the fervor and strength of his ancestors before him.

With a hope and a vision of a future that had never before existed on the farm, he was looking forward to developing unique plans and implementing fresh ideas. This would be the beginning of a new dream to make things better than they had ever been before. He had sacrificed his steady job to take over the farm, which meant he was laying the foundation for a new chapter of his life. With a family of four boys and a wife to take care of, this was not going to be a small undertaking.

The reason I had come was not only to see the farm and all the work generations had put together for his inheritance, but also to offer the help of my three daughters, who would soon begin selling apples and other fruit at the local farmers' market in the region. While he had pickers and others to tend to the orchards, one of his ideas was to expand the financial aspects of the farm by selling his fruit at various markets throughout the state, instead of just the little market stand where his father and grandfather had been selling for years. Ultimately, he wanted to establish a standard of quality by having the best fruit to offer neighbors, friends, and the community at large.

Farmer's Market circa fall 2015 – Smith girls

Not only did I love the idea he had presented to me weeks before, but I was also excited for my daughters to have an opportunity to learn how to run a market booth. Communicating with customers, handling money, and being accountable to inventory were just a few of the lessons they would learn. What I really wanted for my girls was the ability to learn what it means to work for a living and gain skills that would accompany them for the rest of their lives. They were young, ages 7, 8, and 11, but I have always felt that one can never be too young to learn these irreplaceable skills and life lessons.

As Farmer Pyne excitedly guided me toward the large building, I began to understand the enormity of what he was trying to accomplish. Once inside, he was eager to show me all that he had built, which included a gigantic cooler on the right-hand side within the structure that was to replace a much smaller version in a neighboring city. If he was going to expand his offerings as planned, he needed to increase his space and provide a better environment to house his fruit, especially the apples. The stacks of empty bins and crates that lined the inner walls would soon be filled with a variety of fruit, and from what I could see, there was plenty of room to drive his forklift throughout the building, to manage the movement of crates and bins as needed.

Farmer Pyne also showed me an idea that would offer year-round production, using crops from the previous season that had been carefully preserved in his redesigned facility. After crushing these preserved apples into a sweet, all-natural nectar, a drink machine would churn his cider into a delectable slushy drink for the summer months before the real market season would begin. It was refreshing, being made with apple juice and nothing else. This would allow him to offer a much more natural option to quenching one's thirst on a hot summer day than the sugary drinks that were then being offered. Ultimately there would be no wasted time throughout the year as he had proved that he could be selling something all year long.

Soon after, we ventured outside, where he showed me the heavenly white nectarine trees, which were the most amazing nectarines I had ever tasted! As we wandered through the groves of trees, I could see every variety, from tiny saplings to more than 50-year-old trees that had borne the weight of thousands of apples, peaches, nectarines and cherries over the years.

Of all the fruit that was present, his most prized trees were those that bore his apples. The coveted apple was truly the symbol of strength to the entire orchard, as well as the very logo that represented Pyne Farms' label and brand.

I admired the rows of apple trees that ranged from colors of solid red to yellows, greens, and every mix in between. Farmer Pyne was also very excited to show me an apple called the "Elliott," which was a mix between a Golden Delicious and a Starking Delicious apple and was discovered locally in Provo, Utah, by Farmer Grant Elliott.[1]

The story goes that Farmer Elliott found a sapling that began to grow in a remote part of his orchard around 1980. To see how it would do, he placed some rocks around it and let it continue to grow for several years. Within five years it began to produce blossoms, so he allowed a neighbor to graft it into other trees, and the branches began to produce a new variety of apple that was like the Golden Delicious in color, with a slight blush of pink. The Elliott is a tart variety of apple that was recently used in 2021 by Mountain West Hard Cider Company to create a new hard cider called Elliott Gold.[2]

What fascinated me the most about hearing this story of the Elliott apple from Kent was not the fact that it was a new variety, but I had no idea that the odds of creating a new variety of apple were one in 100,000. In other words, a person cannot take the seed from his or her favorite apple and plant it, expecting it to someday grow into a beautiful tree, bearing the much-loved fruit. There is a lot of work that goes into growing an apple tree, and Farmer Pyne was ever so willing to educate me on the dedication necessary to bear such fruit.

In my mind, I began to see a unique correlation to my own career and the role I have had in educating companies all over the country on how to improve their hiring process. The Hiring Tree concept began to take root, and I realized that this same commitment and enthusiasm portrayed by Farmer Pyne is the effort required by an organization to find and hire the right people.

In my world as a hiring expert, I specialize in helping organizations with their hiring processes and practices. For many years, I have helped thousands of organizations look differently at their strategic operations as they relate to hiring and onboarding the right talent. While I have recommended principles found within this book for many years, the hardest part has always been to watch individuals squander the knowledge given. Without proper application, organizations will continue to do what they have always done, with little to no success. The biggest challenge has always been how to motivate and inspire, but more importantly, how to persuade others to be bold and daring enough to put these principles into practice.

As I continued to watch Farmer Pyne peel back the leaves to reveal the different types of apples on his trees, I suddenly realized that the best way to teach others was to do it the way Farmer Pyne was teaching me about apples. When he was peeling those leaves back to reveal the fruit, the analogy became clear. For all of us in the hiring world, the leaves and fruit represent applicants who apply for our open positions. The *leaves* on the tree are applicants who are unqualified or unfit for the position, while the *fruit* represents the actual applicants we wish to pick and move to the bin to be managed in the facility.

After sifting through the myriad of leaves to find the actual fruit, the apples are then gathered and made available for sorting, which involves separating the good fruit from the bad fruit. This process takes additional time, because while the fruit has been picked, not all apples are fit to be placed in front of customers for sale. The customers in this scenario are just the hiring managers or executive team members who are there to select which candidates they wish to hire.

I jokingly shared this idea with Farmer Pyne. In that moment, he taught me something that I will never forget. He said, "We all seek the fruit, but we cannot forget that it all starts with the roots of the tree and the very ground in which the tree is planted." In other words, while organizations are constantly seeking the right applicant to fill their open roles, all too often they forget the *beginning* of the process, which starts at the very roots of what I call the Hiring Tree. Before we can start with the branches of the tree, where the fruit is picked, we must remember where the tree actually begins.

The roots hold the tree in the ground to provide a steady and strengthened system designed to withstand the weather and other dangers that lurk above the ground. If the roots are not properly cared for, the nutrition that provides strength and girth to the main trunk is not given. This will have an immediate impact on the vitamins and minerals sent to the branches. Without these roots securely planted in the ground, the trunk will never grow strong enough to sustain the tree when storms or other elements threaten its livelihood. For an organization, the storms that come may come in the form of new laws, political changes, inflation, economic factors, natural disasters, or even pandemics.

COVID-19 and all the ensuing challenges that have accompanied it, represents the third hiring recession that I have experienced in my professional career. Much like the storms an apple tree can face, this pandemic was a danger lurking above the ground, which a lot of employers were not prepared to face. Like with any recession, the ways in which things were done before the storm arrived are forever changed. Typical of any recession, there is no question that there were some distinct differences, but the principles introduced in this book will continue to hold true in any recessive period.

This is important to understand because as a company begins to develop its own Hiring Tree to help with managing the talent sourcing process, the organization will also find that taking care of the whole tree is crucial to its success. Otherwise, the fruit it desires will never properly develop. When a tree does not bear fruit, it is eventually chopped down and made into firewood.

With that in mind, let's move on to the first principle of the Hiring Tree.

ESTABLISHING THE
FOUNDATIONAL ROOTS

FARMER PYNE would be the first to point out that, while he personally works his farm to ensure the best quality possible, he cannot do it alone. The success of his farm is based heavily on contributions from family, friends, and coworkers, who take on a variety of tasks to fulfill their own roles by following his leadership. This team effort makes all the difference before the blossoms of the spring season even begin to explode from the branches of the trees. With this in mind, in order for these blossoms to burst forth, special care must be taken during the winter months to provide health and longevity to the root systems of the trees.

The initial growth of a young sapling is based on one of three unique root structures that will follow a season-specific growth pattern to support the developing tree. An apple tree specifically uses a complex system called a "taproot," which is vital to its firmness, its absorption of sustenance, and its continued growth as it begins its journey to becoming a fruitful contributor to the orchard. The taproot is the first root type and is deep enough to reach into the moisture reserves of the soil to sustain the tree when there is a scarcity of vitamins and minerals, or even during times of drought (which, in Utah, is a common occurrence, due to the desert-like nature of the region). Over time, the depth of the taproots can reach downward up to 20 feet, serving as anchors to plant the tree firmly in place.

The second root type, known as "fibrous roots," will stem from the taproots to grasp nutrients horizontally. Fibrous roots also provide an outreach for stability and balance, since their stretching arms expand three to five feet below the soil and sometimes hundreds of feet outward. Being fairly deep within the soil, they oftentimes will miss out on nutrients that can be found near the surface, which is why the last root type is a vital team member.

The final root type, called the "feeder roots," grows from the fibrous roots, extending their reach upward. Feeder roots enhance the efforts of the fibrous roots by allowing the reach to "feed" as close to the surface as possible. Feeder roots are small but mighty in what they bring to the root system as a whole. In most cases, their exertions occur only a few millimeters from the topsoil. These roots can be likened to the worker ants of an ant colony; they provide the majority of oxygen and water absorption, and they compete with other shrubs and plants in seeking out much-needed vitamins and nutrients.

The taproot system of an apple tree teaches us a fundamental concept in developing a Hiring Tree, which must rely on the entire team in order to be successful. All three root types must work together to achieve the overall objective, by feeding off one another in their supportive efforts. The first principle learned from this example is to recognize that at its roots, the hiring process is, and always will be, a team effort. The three root types described herein can be compared to the very foundation that must be found within all organizations in their efforts to hire new employees. These employees will help to expand the business, as well as increase revenue, which then leads to the growth desired. If these roots are not firmly planted, which can only be accomplished by working together, then the very foundation of growing the organization will fail.

The three root systems of the apple tree are easily compared to the core setup of an organization. The taproots represent the first members of the hiring team: the executives or C-Suite individuals. This team also establishes the defined mission, values, and what I call the "why" of the company's existence. The fibrous roots represent managers and supervisors who provide stability and strength to represent and fulfill the "why" of the organization. Finally, the feeder roots represent all other employees, who, much like the worker ants, are doing the majority of the work to ensure the success of the company as a whole, thus bringing the "why" to fruition.

The next three chapters will dig deeper into how to better establish these roots in a way that will provide an excellent source of nutrients for the future of a fruit-bearing Hiring Tree.

2

TAP INTO THE ROOTS

JUST LIKE THE DEPTH of the taproot of an apple tree provides foundational strength, understanding this sturdy part of the root system for the Hiring Tree of an organization is the only way to establish a firm base, allowing the other two root systems to work in harmony.

The taproot starts with the executives and high-level members of an organization responsible for establishing the company culture. One of the biggest failures I find in many organizations, as they begin this process of establishing their own Hiring Tree, involves a struggle for support and confidence from the executive leadership. As leaders, these individuals must recognize the part they play, since the taproot of a well-established Hiring Tree is the only way to ensure continued success in attracting more talent.

Those who find themselves in these key roles must accept that they are the steady heartbeat that all others will depend upon. Just like all roots of an apple tree must connect to the taproot, the grassroots effort, and the dedication of all employees of an organization, will have no effect on hiring if the connection to leadership is weak. Through the years, I have seen companies fail, and ultimately go out of business, due to this fundamental lack of connection.

How does an organization develop this connection? It begins to be established through what most organizations call a "mission statement." A mission statement defines the overall objective and purpose as to why the organization exists to begin with. Smaller companies and startup organizations oftentimes struggle with this concept, because in some cases, they are still trying to find themselves amidst the chaos of building and establishing the company itself. However, having been part of the creation and growth of multiple organizations since starting my career, I have discovered that every founder starts the business for a reason. There is a driving motivation as to why they decided to uproot themselves from any previous endeavors to begin the journey that becomes the organization they run. The reasons for creating such an organization can be modified, expanded upon, or change over time, but they are always present. Even if it seems basic at first in the way it is described, the mission of an organization must exist and must be clearly defined and written out. Just like a ship in the darkness relies on the light from a single tower upon the shoreline, a company needs to have a beacon to look to in order to steer its efforts in a consistent direction.

The next step in ensuring this connection to the taproot is to establish a set of core values. Core values are so important because they provide a written definition of an established set of principles that all must follow, providing support to the mission as a whole. As the organization continues to grow and establish itself as a viable entity, certain rules and regulations are introduced to help the organization govern itself. Employees learn the rules, but more importantly they learn that the core values and overall mission of the company guide the reason for the obedience to these rules. Rules should never restrict employees from finding success and fulfillment in their roles, and these rules should never detract from the core values and mission of the organization.

In the Christian world, there is a story of a man named Moses, whose experience helps to paint a picture as to what this might look like. The goal (think "mission statement") for Moses was to lead the people to the Promised Land. It was simple and straightforward. To help with this mission, a law (think "core values") was established with two simple parts: love God and love thy neighbor. If there were any questions as to the mission, the Israelites could refer to the core values, which provided clarity and guidance on their journey.

Unfortunately, as the Israelites began their journey, trouble ensued regarding what it meant to follow the law of love. This delay led to the establishment of a set of rules, known as the Ten Commandments, written in stone by God himself to further clarify the two core values of loving God and loving thy neighbor. The first four commandments defined what it meant to love God. The final six commandments defined what it meant to love thy neighbor. Consequences were set forth, and all were expected to follow the rules, which were guided by the core values, so all could safely accomplish the mission.

Every organization needs a set of rules *and* principles that direct all actions. When employees make decisions based on established principles, as defined by the core values, it helps guide them in their efforts.

Rules often have a bad connotation caused by dictatorship and enforcement. This is ascribable to the actions of a power-hungry, unconfident leader, who takes advantage of rules to exercise control over others, often due to the lack of control existent in the individual.

When a rule is broken, there is an established consequence for violating the rule, but this should not give license to unforgiving leadership. It saddens me when I see some organizations that are so top heavy on rules and violations, that employees feel choked and unable to fulfill their roles in a productive and positive way. In other words, the principle has been trumped by the rule, allowing no room for error. This type of environment is not conducive to establishing an effective Hiring Tree to help with growth, because it does not allow the employees to connect with their leaders in a genuine way. While rules are there to protect from previous mistakes or lessons learned along the way, it is important to have a way to educate newcomers without causing harm to morale and strategy.

The key is to help employees understand and embrace the fact that the rules are tied to the principles, which are designed to protect them from the negative consequences that could possibly follow.

In a discussion with Farmer Pyne on this subject of rules, he reminded me that the laws of nature are not very forgiving. In other words, there are extreme consequences that result from disobeying the rules, but this does not mean that, as a leader, his enforcement of those rules should be overbearing or detrimental to his team or orchard. His father taught him how to effectively deal with the laws of nature by being prepared and by taking action to prevent problems in the first place. By consistently following a set of farming principles at certain times of the year, there were ways to avoid, or counter, the effects of nature that threatened the roots every day.

While rules must exist, care must be taken to not allow rules to restrict the actions of others. I love the example he used to describe this concept for me, which helped me understand what he meant by this restriction.

When it comes to protecting the roots, Farmer Pyne often jests about these little creatures, called gophers, that dig into the ground on the farm. Gophers do not compete for the nutrients sought after by the trees, but they do love to eat the taproots of an apple tree. When this part of the tree is damaged or destroyed, the tree will not survive.

There are a variety of ways to remove gophers from the farm, providing a set of rules to follow to eradicate the issue. One example is to set a trap to catch them. While effective, it can be difficult to lure them out of their underground network of tunnels. Another rule of thumb is that gophers are territorial, and for some reason, they do not attract a lot of friends. In other words, you only have to deal with one at a time, and not a bunch of them at once.

In order to lure them out of their burrow, one method is to flood their underground matrix to scare them out. The principle here is to force them to leave the area. But too much water can damage the tree roots as well, so care must be taken when using this method. It was very enlightening to me that, while the rule itself was a good practice, the same rule could be taken too far and cause unintentional damage, limiting the roots' ability to absorb the nutrients needed.

For any organization looking to create their own set of principles for the first time, it is important to remember that these core values should be seen as flexible, in order to establish a guide for all employees to follow. As rules begin to surface, they should never be so concrete that they put a limitation on progress or lead to additional harm, like the flooding of gopher burrows.

I love this quote, which illustrates this perfectly, spoken by Joseph Smith in 1851 when asked how he was able to manage so many diverse groups of people from a variety of countries, backgrounds, and languages: "I teach them correct principles, and they govern themselves."[3]

Allow core values to be the principles taught by the leadership team, and then allow employees to govern themselves within the bounds that have been set.

For organizations looking to modify core values or add to what they currently have in place, I recommend contemplating whether those changes are more of a guide or if they are meant to control and dominate. While Farmer Pyne knows he needs to flood the gophers' living area to keep them from damaging the taproot, he also cannot allow the area to become overly flooded so that it causes the other roots of the system to drown.

However, gophers that constantly want to eat away at the taproot *must* be removed. The greatest example I have seen in business might be a toxic employee, who does not ascribe to the core values or mission of an organization, and continually attacks the company at the very roots upon which it is founded. Like the gopher, this can cause a great disconnect between the taproot and the other roots of the system, gnawing away at what was once a firm, interlocking relationship. Is it any wonder that these individuals do not have a lot of friends, much like the gopher? In an organizational setting, many individuals who act like the gopher will find, very quickly, that they will no longer fit in.

Ultimately, a solid Hiring Tree that will continue to produce hires for an organization, starts with this taproot connection where managers and supervisors are confident and connected with their C-suite leadership. The reason this connection must be in place first, is because the managers and supervisors of the organization will have this same type of connection with the rest of the employees.

It is important to recognize that no one wants to follow poor leadership, which may cause managers and supervisors to disengage. When leadership styles from the executives are not effective at *conveying* the message about the core values and mission of the organization, managers and supervisors will struggle to *deliver* that message, creating a disconnect which is like gnawing away at the root. The executive team should be intentional and authentic when working with managers, since the delegation of the rules fall on the shoulders of this supervisory group. When the overall vision is understood, the executive team will recognize that the best way to do a job may not always the look the same for everyone. The principles will be followed because they will govern themselves within the boundaries of what has been taught and modeled.

An old Chinese proverb I heard years ago has always stuck with me about how important this can be. It states: "Keep company with good men, and good men you will imitate." If managers and supervisors do not have the right leadership to imitate, the message can be distorted, misunderstood, or ignored altogether. Like the gophers in the apple orchard, managers may begin to eat away at the taproot of the Hiring Tree when they are not engaged and trained properly, making it difficult to attract new talent. The managers, or "fibrous roots," must be led by example and come together to form an unbreakable bond. I love that the next part of the root system is described as fibrous, because the term "fiber," as defined in the next chapter, helps illustrate the importance of this bond.

MANAGE FIBER INTAKE

FIBER IS SUCH AN IMPORTANT PART of the digestive system in the human body because it helps to regulate the body's use of sugars, ultimately keeping hunger and blood sugar in check. Fiber is a type of carbohydrate that the body *cannot* digest. Most carbohydrates can be easily broken down into tiny sugar molecules, known as glucose. However, fiber *cannot be broken down* into these sugar molecules and will pass through the body undigested. Since fiber can help regulate hunger and blood sugar, fiber intake is such an important part of a healthy diet. Apples are a great source of soluble fiber, which can help lower glucose levels and help lower blood cholesterol.

The managers and supervisors of an organization represent the fibrous roots of the taproot system. The fibrous roots from an apple tree sprout from the main taproot of the tree to seek out nutrients needed to help the tree grow and provide stability as they fan out from the base. These roots when bound together, create a connection that is unbreakable, much like fiber in food. The goal of the fibrous roots is to expand the reach of the taproots, which begin the process of collecting vital nutrients from the soil to help the tree begin its growth upward. This growth of the tree will establish the right trunk strength and girth to begin creating the branches, which growth leads to the delectable fruit!

Protection from the gopher must occur through the example of the leadership team as described in the previous chapter. This will give the fibrous roots a fighting chance at establishing a base structure that is firm, expanding the root system beyond the elongated stretch downward by the main carrot-like taproot. I have always thought of it like an umbrella slowly opening up. These fibrous roots will expand and produce the much smaller feeder roots that will absorb water, minerals, and other vitamins to send to the core of the system as the tree begins its climb above the ground. The fibrous roots are much bigger, and thus have much more power than the feeder roots, but again, they must connect fully to the taproot, or the life of the tree will be lost.

Obviously, the analogy here is that much like the fibrous roots, organizational managers and supervisors who are fully connected to the executive team will find success as they expand their reach to grow the organization.

It is important to remember that the growth of an organization is more than just the *number* of employees. Growth includes all aspects of the business. From the service or product provided, to the customer and clients acquired and retained, everything adds up to create a firmly rooted system that the branches of an organization's Hiring Tree will depend upon to attract new employees as this expansion continues.

Ultimately, there must be a solid relationship between the managers and supervisors and the executive team. This fibrous group of individuals must ascribe to the mission, core values, and the rules, as established by the tap-rooted executives. These core leaders must also recognize three core characteristics: they are vital to the distribution of the rules; they are the exemplars of the core values; and they act as beacons to the mission of the company. Managers and supervisors are empowered by the executive team to embody these three core characteristics of the organization.

Over the years I have seen countless statistics, surveys, and other forms of information gathering that show how important clear direction, gratitude, recognition, genuine compassion, meaningful relationships, and company culture are to *all* organizations. A lack of direction is a misunderstanding of the mission statement. Negative company culture is often tied to a lack of core values that guide, motivate, and direct action. This leads to a lack of trust and little to no transparency, which is why rules are broken and many star employees experience burnout as they pick up the slack of others. This environment then leads to most employees feeling disconnected, disengaged, and apathetic. There is rarely recognition of a job well done, and gratitude and empathy do not exist. Just like the root system of an apple tree, in this scenario, the gophers win, the taproot withers away, and the tree collapses in on itself.

The most detailed statistic I have seen comes from an old colleague of mine who works for Gallup. He shared the data with me several years ago. In a 2017 poll of over one million US workers,[4] the number one reason employees left their most recent position was due to a disconnect and negative experience with their boss or immediate supervisor. Close to seventy-five percent admitted in the survey that this lack of leadership and guidance was why they left their previous employer.

In my own research on the same subject for the past fourteen years, this statistic holds true during a recession, as well as during an economic boom. There are a variety of bad leadership types I have seen throughout my years of consulting with thousands of organizations in hundreds of industries. I think it is important to describe some of these bad examples, in order to recognize the most common reasons individuals are selected to manage or supervise others.

When choosing a manager or supervisor, many organizations

make the mistake of selecting individuals who are unqualified for the role. Why is this blunder made? It boils down to the *reason* the person was hired for this important role in the first place. Too many organizations hire a manager based on tenure, popularity, desperate need, or lack of candidates to choose from. Part of this stems from lack of growth in the roles within the organization. In fact, many employees might see the prospect of becoming a manager as the only option to move up in their careers and possibly make more money. The challenge with this environment is that it attracts the wrong mentality for someone to move into such a role, and oftentimes these are the wrong reasons for someone to vie for the position in the first place.

This is also why it is so crucial to think about the pay structures, compensation, and benefits in the organization and how they can impact employees' desires to move laterally instead of upward. In the root system of a tree, it is a lateral growth that produces the greatest stability, thus creating a solid example of the type of growth that must exist within a company to avoid some of these pitfalls in selecting leaders incorrectly.

In my experience, the best way to measure the potential success of someone in a supervisory or managerial position is through scientifically validated assessments, which, in some states, may also need to go through an additional "bias audit."[5] These assessments will measure what is not seen about the individual in their current role, and they are not based on what might be found on a résumé or employee review.

The potential for leaders within an organization does exist, which is why this is not something that needs to be left to chance. I have often heard the comment, "I went with my gut." Unfortunately, it is quite rare that the gut is a valid predictor of success. The use of the gut needs to be left to digestion, not decision-making.

This approach is not an objective way to decide, either,

because those making the internal decisions tend to focus on contenders who think and act just like they do. This can be detrimental to diversity in the role, to the development of new ideas, and to the prospect of having a true leader, who can take on the challenges, burdens, and enthusiasm needed for this type of leadership role. I often speak with decision-makers who tell me that they liked someone because of the way they thought, the way they dressed, the way they acted in the interview (which is an act anyway), and the way in which they agreed with everything the interviewer commented or shared.

Just like the fibrous roots must dig deeper and spread out to establish balance for the tree, assessments help the interviewer find the right fit for this type of role by digging deeper into how successful this person will be when such a mantle of responsibility is placed upon him or her. It also allows the manager being considered for the role to understand their own strengths, which can empower them to succeed because they will better understand how to manage in their own way. This is important because, ultimately, there is no one ideal way to manage.

The most successful managers are those that are taught to recognize their own strengths, as well as the strengths of the employees they manage, and then act upon those strengths. A focus on weaknesses will never produce the results desired in employee engagement, culture, or relationships with coworkers and clients. By focusing on the strengths of the individual instead of their weaknesses, this produces confidence in the manager, strengthening the connection with the mission, core values, and the *why* behind the rules of the organization.

Here are a few real-life examples for contemplation, describing potential qualities and styles to avoid. If these leaders do exist in the organization, it may be best to find ways to retrain, to reestablish the right connections, or perhaps to find ways to let the gopher go to another orchard. What I relate in these situations happened to people I know. Names have been changed for ethical reasons, but they illustrate quite effectively areas where some mid-level leaders have failed in their responsibilities to be the fibrous part of the root system.

Superiority Complex

Felicia achieved great success in her role as a physician's nurse, which lasted for the better part of three years. Her physician, who was also her direct boss, absolutely appreciated the role she played in making sure charts were pulled and ready for clinic days, so the days ran smoothly, and the doctor could focus on the patients' needs and truly care for their health.

The working relationship between Felicia and the doctor had become solid enough that the symmetry between them had attracted new patients due to steady referrals from grateful clients who were happy to share their experience with others. Felicia even had the opportunity to relay feedback and share ideas with her boss on how to more effectively accomplish other tasks and aspects of the business, which contributed to additional success and growth.

The parent company recognized the connection that existed in Felicia's office and decided to develop a way to implement this unity in their other offices. To this end, a new nurse manager was then assigned to the office to work with all the nurses at the various clinic locations. The new manager, in an effort to get all of the clinics on the same page, decided to review some of the rules where the doctors had been a little relaxed in their enforcement. She made a checklist of all the rules, visited with each nurse at the various locations, and had frank conversations addressing areas of improvement.

After meeting with Felicia, the manager wrote her up for three perceived infractions: excessive decorating during the holidays, bringing her kitten to the office one time six months earlier to share with coworkers, and not wearing scrubs on non-clinic days when no patients were in the office. The manager told her that if these adjustments could not be made or complied with, she may want to consider finding work elsewhere. The new manager mentioned to Felicia that she herself had had to make a similar decision to leave a job once, emphasizing why she left.

At the close of the review, the new manager reminded Felicia that the work she did was top notch and that there were no complaints about her work ethic and ability to get the job done.

In this scenario, the new manager missed an incredible opportunity to develop the "unity" desired by the parent company. So, what went wrong? This is the first manager-type that I see exist in many workplaces: those put into a position of power, who forget where they came from. They take the newly found power and exercise it in a compulsory way to enforce rules, without focusing on the principles and core values of the organization, but instead, focus on nit-picky habits or quirks the employee may have. Often, these are little complaints or mistakes from long ago that have been since forgotten. Sometimes, the rules enforced, or situations brought up as a concern, are not even relevant to the role itself and the employee's ability to accomplish the tasks assigned. This managerial style fails to focus on the *strengths* of the employee to build upon the foundation established. There is no attempt at a genuine relationship of trust, but rather that of an "I am better than you" attitude because of a title.

When my daughters first started working for Farmer Pyne, I was amazed at his ability to focus on each of their strengths to help them succeed in running a market. Some mistakes made meant that he made less money in that transaction, but he only focused on the mistake long enough to teach the lesson. His ability to move forward with an enthusiasm in what they could accomplish inspired them to work harder and smarter. With this training in place, my middle daughter Ruby has been so successful that she has improved the revenue of her market location for the last eight years, always making more money than the year before. Ruby's methods have even been used at other markets to create similar improvements.

The best way to address a leader that tends to see the little problems is to focus their training on what is most important. It is critical to help them understand that the overall goal and objective is to find ways to improve the organization, which will require a shift in focus. This improvement should be directly tied to the performance, or lack thereof, by those employees involved. Leaders like this need extensive training on separating good work ethic from personal quirks and preferences of the individual worker that are not relevant to job performance. In this example, the very issues Felicia was cited for as problems may have correlated directly to the success the office was experiencing that differentiated them from the other clinics.

Personal Fear and Doubt

Bill had recently been promoted to a supervisory role over a group of individuals in a manufacturing plant which designed steering mechanism parts for tractors. His promotion occurred six weeks after starting in a new department for the organization. Bill expressed to me how uncertain he was about how to manage others but was eager to impress those who were above him.

One of his subordinates came to him with a concern about a mechanical tool they used, citing that it seemed to have a slight flaw that caused it to shake when attaching one piece to another. Bill listened to the situation half-heartedly since he had a similar experience with the same tool prior to his promotion.

Unfortunately, Bill was very nervous and apprehensive about bringing up this issue to the executive team. He feared that, though important to *one* employee, it might not be as important to the company or those to whom he reported. The executive team had recently given Bill this role and was very firm about focusing on specific results. Bill decided to play it safe by letting the employee know that the issue would be brought up in a meeting with the executives. Bill mentioned to me that, at first, he failed to tell his executives for several weeks because he was unsure how to bring it up with them, since he had also reported the same issue prior to his promotion.

The employee continued to nag Bill for several months to check in on how things were going, only to be told that nothing could be done just yet. Shortly after a *fifth* reminder on the matter, Bill received a distressing call from the team. The employee who had been proactive about addressing the issue had been hospitalized due to losing a finger from a faulty mechanism on the tool in question.

As the employee shared his side of the story with me, it was difficult to listen between the sobs and sniffles, as he relived this horrific experience. I will never forget how he felt, citing that, because Bill was so focused on following orders and maintaining his image with those above him, there was no loyalty to the team of individuals in Bill's realm of responsibility. The opportunity to avoid a disastrous situation went unanswered, led to a life-changing result, and left a team of individuals questioning the integrity of their new leader.

What's worse is that many teammates already knew Bill, because they had worked side by side with him for years before his promotion. In this managerial style, fear takes over, causing a rift to form because of a lack of respect, and no real effort made to fight for the safety, concern, and welfare of those for whom they have a primary responsibility.

A leader must be able to make difficult decisions, even when it may put them in a situation where they feel uncomfortable or unable to sustain the image they are trying to present. In apples, there is a disease called "bitter pit" that can impact the taste of an apple, creating a lack of sweetness to the apple. The affected fruit develop dark spots on the skin, which quickly spread, causing a spectacle of freckles on the fruit that make the apple look sick. I remember well the first time my middle daughter discovered this in several apples we were prepared to sell at the market and addressed the issue with Farmer Pyne.

In these circumstances, Farmer Pyne could pick the rest of the fruit and sell the crop to his customers, but very quickly, the apples will go bad. While only some fruit might have the bitter pit when discovered, the rest of the fruit can still be potentially affected, creating a difficult decision to do away with a lot of fruit that could have produced a bountiful harvest to bring in additional revenue. Farmer Pyne wants to maintain the best fruit in the state, which means this image must be maintained by eliminating the bad fruit even before it looks bad. If a mistake is made, the customer can return the fruit for a refund or a replacement.

I have a deep respect for how Farmer Pyne takes ownership in this issue, striving to be an example to his workers who are there to help him sell the fruit. After my daughter asked about this issue she had discovered that year, he instructed us on how to find this type of disease in the apples to discard them accordingly.

Managers have an obligation to be *leaders*, which means they are also protectors and advocates for those they manage. Part of great leadership requires that the manager listen to employees' complaints, with the purpose of addressing those concerns that legitimately need to be addressed. A manager needs to be trained on how to effectively prioritize those employee voices, to know how to address them in a professional way.

When a manager is trying to maintain an image or to carry out certain actions based on a state of fear, poor and dangerous results may be the ultimate consequences. Where there is personal fear, compassion and concern for safety cannot exist.

Bill felt strongly that he was not prepared to manage others but was excited about the opportunity to prove himself and provide more financial support for his family. He has since received some incredible training with a new company, but the lesson learned from this situation will forever be ingrained in his mind. The one wish he had in sharing his story with me was to express how important he felt being trained on *how* to manage would have alleviated the pain that accompanied this powerful lesson.

I'll Be Watching You

Susan was excited to start a new position as the social media marketing specialist for a midsized insurance company looking to find ways to attract more clients. With so many new programs available, and little to no previous efforts by the company to market these programs, it was going to be a fresh start.

The chief marketing officer (CMO) appeared completely supportive, admitting multiple times that she had never really marketed using social media platforms. Susan had a proven track record of success using social media practices that were considered to be new methods. It was a different medium, with which the current CMO was not familiar.

Before she even started on her first day, Susan began to research the company and the program offerings for the industry, and she developed a plan of action to begin her endeavors to produce immediate results.

Within the first few weeks, the CMO handed Susan a checklist of things to do and developed a plan of action based on what had worked in the past using other marketing channels. Susan was to report to the CMO every week, but after several weeks, the CMO began to check in on the status of the checklist every other day.

Susan discovered quickly that the checklist contained several items that did not work in social media advertising. After bringing this up with the CMO, her boss decided that maybe a daily check-in would be better, to ensure the steps were followed. This would allow the CMO to maintain control over the process in general, which included the budget allocated to the project.

Several months went by as Susan frantically tried to follow the checklist of procedures to please the CMO, while also trying to implement some new ideas. The daily check-ins created additional time constraints, and with little to no additional budget for the project, it was difficult to produce the results desired by the CMO.

Ultimately, the CEO stepped in to let Susan know that the new ideas were not working well, and they could either move her to a different role or accept her resignation.

There were multiple red flags in this scenario, and there is no doubt that micromanaging an employee can be suffocating and debilitating. In this case, there was no opportunity for creativity, which is something Susan thrived on in her previous accomplishments. It can also be demoralizing for employees to be constantly monitored and required to check in on menial tasks that may not even be relevant to the role.

Susan felt that there was absolutely no motivation after several months, and the guidance provided was misdirected in an area that had never been tested before. Her comment on this matter was very revealing: "If the CMO hired me to do a job she did not know how to do, why were there so many nit-picky rules and steps required? At first, I felt she believed in me as a true expert in an area of marketing that had never been done before by the company. The CMO did not know how to use this channel of advertising and admitted it openly. This inspired and motivated me to create what I knew would be a very successful set of campaigns aimed at fulfilling their directive to acquire new customers. Instead, my days were filled with endless hours of checking in. There were even days she would come into the office just to watch what I was doing. I became so nervous and fidgety that I nearly forgot how to do what I was highly capable of doing and what I was hired to accomplish in the first place. I started doubting my own skills in a field where I had previously been very successful."

This type of leader lacks the trust in the skills and knowledge the new employee brings to the table. Oftentimes these leaders will be so focused on the rules or processes and making sure that they are followed, that they leave little room for the employee to accomplish anything.

While it is important to have defined objectives, I have found that creativity is much more productive when failure is allowed. For every failure I have experienced in my career, I have been grateful to leaders who haven't taken it as a sign that I must be followed, overshadowed, and watched at every turn.

There is a famous line in a song that has always truly frightened me, which is why I have often wondered why it is labeled as a "love song": "Every breath you take, every move you make, I'll be watching you."

Oh, how it makes me shudder!

There are times when Farmer Pyne will train new hires to pick the apples in the orchard, which requires a certain amount of patience to keep the apples from bruising. While there are certain principles to follow, if he micromanages his new hires constantly, it slows down the harvest process and creates a nervousness in the employee that only creates additional delays and damage to the fruit. There is no question that some new employees during the learning curve have bruised apples that are now only fit for juicing. Instead of being a "helicopter boss," he allows these failures to become lessons that can be used for teaching proper methods. Sometimes those failures lead to a new idea or method of harvesting more effectively for each individual.

Failure is going to happen when new things are attempted, but it is not always a sign that someone has been ultimately defeated. Trying new things for the first time requires an element of failure, or there would be no need for a learning curve. In this case, good leaders need to be accepting of failure, knowing that failure at a particular task does not make the individual a failure overall.

A good way to help managers in this type of leadership style is to remind them *why* they felt the need to hire this person for the role in the first place. This feeling is rooted in faith that the new hire is highly capable of accomplishing the functions of the role that needs to be fulfilled by the organization. When a manager bases hiring decisions on this conviction, there is no need to micromanage, because there exists an element of trust and confidence that will contribute to the progress of the working relationship between the individual and the manager.

Who's the Boss?

The final example is taken from the annals of American history. It is the story of a man who was an incredible leader, but in his drive to be number one, his pride led to a court-martial for carelessness and disregard for a higher authority. This moment in history is now a contributing scene in the performance of one of my favorite musicals, *Hamilton*. The man's name in this example of poor leadership is Charles Lee.

Lee had a proven track record of success in leadership roles during wartime in Colonial America, so it was no surprise that when the American War for Independence broke out in 1775, he was one of several people appointed to serve. His ambition was to be the commander in chief, a role he lost to a fellow Virginian by the name of George Washington. He was further disappointed when, instead of being the second-in-command, he was assigned the role of major general, which was the third person in line. If this competition had been an Olympic event, Lee basically received the bronze medal when he felt he deserved at least the silver. Luckily, the second-in-command fell ill, leaving the role to Lee after all.

As the Revolutionary War dragged on, Lee began to complain about the actions of Washington as the commander in chief in various letters and correspondence to other generals, as well as the Continental Congress. While Lee was in the very act of writing one of these letters of complaint, he was captured by the British and became a prisoner of war for a short time.

Once released, Lee rendezvoused with Washington at Valley Forge, Pennsylvania, during the winter months of 1778. Upon arrival, Lee noted the troops assigned to him appeared to be incapable of battle due to their unhealthy state. Lee quickly jumped to his own conclusion on the matter, accusing Washington of poor leadership based on two major losses against the British, which had occurred earlier. He even rallied others to agree with him that, politically, Washington should be relieved of his role as commander in chief.

Lee was so focused on what he felt was a lack in Washington's character, that he failed to recognize the efforts Washington was making at Valley Forge to retrain and prepare the troops for the next battle. Lee also failed to notice the deficiency in support from Congress to provide food and supplies, which led to the dismal state of the troops. In some cases, supplies had been thwarted by the British, and with the severity of the winter during those six months prior to Lee's arrival, many troops and horses lost their lives.

Shortly after Lee arrived in Valley Forge, there was an array of battles, which led to the Battle at Monmouth Court House in June 1778. A specific battle plan was outlined and agreed upon at a convened council that included most of the American generals, but as soon as Washington left, Lee disobeyed orders and devised a different plan.

When executed, Lee's plan turned the tide of the battle so heavily in favor of the British army, that Lee called a retreat in an effort to save the rest of the troops under his poorly coordinated attack. Lee's insubordination and disregard for Washington's leadership and command led to the common theme of "retreat" as shouted by Lee in the play. Lee also failed to report the retreat, which limited Washington in his ability to execute the original plan as the battle ensued, leading to many unnecessary casualties.

I love this example, because Lee felt he should have been the one in charge when it was not his role to command, nor was it his right to change the plans agreed upon. Lee argued that he saved many lives due to the retreat but failed to recognize that his "shameful"[6] retreat may not have been necessary had he followed the command given by Washington in the first place. The biggest mistake was when Lee cast the blame on Washington entirely, completely undermining the one who was in charge. Lee also gave himself full credit for what little success existed.

Just like the fibrous roots of the tree are not to take on the role of the taproots, this type of leader must recognize the role they play without undermining the authority of those above them. The ego of this type of leader causes them to think they are better than those in a higher position of power. Armed with pride, this type of leader will often go so far as to create their own rules, abandoning the core values and principles established by the executive team, elevating themselves into their own position of power, and will often seek the support of others within the organization to accompany them on their misaligned desire for power. All leaders have a part to play in the root system, but assuming others' roles in this process will sever the connections needed to establish the success of the feeder roots (the employees).

Abundant Thinking

One of the most successful concepts I have seen that is a counterbalance to a power-hungry leader, is a principle called "abundant thinking." There are a variety of definitions to this concept, but in essence it is the opposite of scarcity thinking.

In selling apples, scarcity thinking forces the sales rep to focus on the next paycheck or a desired bonus. When a new customer approaches, the rep may even fight or argue with other sales reps to take the lead. It is an egotistical approach because it does not focus on the customer and their favorite apple, but the focus is on the salesperson who is trying to convince the buyer to go with a different apple altogether that may not even be a fit. For example, I would never sell a sweet apple to someone who wishes to make an apple pie. Sweet apples will get mushy while being cooked, so the better option is to use a tarter apple that will maintain its shape, creating a much better pie.

Human resource professionals have experienced these kinds of scarcity sales calls and attitudes where the primary focus is to complete the sale regardless of the needs of the company. These types of calls are then avoided, and the salesperson may find that they struggle to get a hold of the contact going forward.

Abundant thinking is selfless, believing that the universe has plenty to offer everyone. Sharing knowledge and teaching skills to others is a great way to move everyone in the same direction of improvement. To illustrate an example, we can look at a grove of apple trees being taken care of by the farmer.

All the trees in the orchard are seeking to absorb nutrients, while Farmer Pyne is watering and spraying vitamins and minerals, creating an abundance, so that the trees do not necessarily have to compete with one another. Abundant thinking is knowing and accepting the fact that there is enough available for all, so that, when a new tree is introduced into the orchard, the other trees are not going to attack the new tree and keep it from enjoying what is made readily available by the farmer. There is no need for other trees to feel threatened by the introduction of new trees into the orchard, thus creating a mentality of abundant thinking where there is a desire and willingness to share what is being provided for all.

In my experience at ApplicantPro, I have learned how critical this concept can be to the growth of an organization. The reason this is so important is because as an organization grows, the roles of individuals must be passed on to others. When we started ApplicantPro, Ryan and I were basically in charge of marketing, sales, customer support, graphics, cancellations, collections, and other aspects of the business. As we began to grow, Ryan was very adamant about the need to create a process that could be duplicated repeatedly, which in the Human Resources world is called "succession planning" where skills and knowledge can be passed on to the next person in the role without fear of letting that part of the process go.

Ryan taught me that the most important aspect of abundant thinking is to be confident enough to train someone else to become better than the teacher. One year I created a process to contact current clients to find ways to help them by providing information about additional products and services we offered. I was able to prove the success of the program by producing more than a million dollars in revenue over the course of eighteen months. The program was so successful that it turned into an entirely new department called "client success," with a focus on educating clients on what they were missing, which led to the purchase of additional products and services.

It was an incredible accomplishment for me personally. I worked hard and documented everything. I felt a renewed sense of purpose in my role, and the process itself was focused on how to help our clients succeed, which is something I ascribe to. It had an impact on multiple departments and coworkers. After all this effort, I was asked to give up the client success department entirely to a new team leader who was to take over the process and implement the concept companywide.

I could have been angry that I was not asked to be the team

lead for what started out as a department of one. While the temptation to be bitter lingered for a bit, I was reminded of our core value of abundant thinking as exemplified by Ryan, my leader. There were plenty of other clients that had a need of more services and products. I was only one person, and I could never have contacted all of them on my own. The new department created new leadership opportunities for current employees, new positions for job seekers, and an incredible experience for *all* of our clients. Passing on this knowledge and training has led to the success of thousands of people. It would have been selfish of me to not share my success with others. I marvel at my current team members that are in this department because they have taken this program far beyond what I could have ever imagined. Their success is my success, and I am grateful to hear their experiences that continue to empower our clients every day to improve their hiring processes.

This thought process of sharing is prevalent because rather than focusing on what one doesn't have, the focus is on what one *does* have. Due to a consistent expression of gratitude, there is a realization that there is enough available to want others to enjoy the same. This allows employees to establish the correct connection with their leaders, which also leads to loyalty and longevity.

Abundant thinking is the fiber that leaders need to regulate the company and provide a pattern of succession planning across all areas of the business. Much like the fiber in a healthy diet, it cannot be broken down, but acts as a regulator to stop the negative effects of bad leadership and help leaders stay in check. Where there is abundance, all succeed, and all find joy and fulfillment in that success. The fibrous roots of an apple tree help the feeder roots find success in their efforts to bring in the right nutrients to feed the whole tree, efforts which are the focus of our next chapter.

FEEDING FRENZY:
The Most Industrious Roots

I WANT TO RETURN to a concept introduced in the second chapter for a brief moment, because there is a second threat that exists above the ground, from which the roots of an apple tree *must* be protected. This preservation has to do with the shrubs, weeds, and other shallow-rooted turf that may rob the roots of sufficient nutrient absorption. These intruders can make it difficult for the feeder roots to provide nourishment to the root system as a whole.

For a young sapling, this is vital to the survival of the tree, especially at the beginning of its growth process. Once again, special care must be taken to eradicate this shrubbery from the surface so that the feeder roots do not have to compete for nutrients. Farmer Pyne stated that the key here is a steady, persistent approach. Consistency on a scheduled basis is best, to make certain that the weeds and shrubbery do not get so out of hand that they become a burden to manage. In fact, the smaller the shrubs and weeds, the easier it is to mow and cut things back, thus maintaining the desired control. Left unattended, especially during the summer months, the weeds can become unruly due to their ability to grow very quickly.

By keeping these intruders at bay, the feeder roots are able to grow upward within inches of the surface, without having to be so competitive in their efforts to feed the root system itself.

As mentioned previously, the feeder roots are the most important part of the system, to allow longevity and overall growth; otherwise, the tree can be stunted in its production and will not generate fruit. Since these roots can be found much closer to the surface, care also must be taken above the ground when watering, spraying for critters, and cutting back the weeds.

In this analogy, the feeder roots are the employees, which do represent the most important parts of the taproot system. If employees are not seen as the most important asset an organization has, the "gophers, weeds, and insects" will take over, making it very difficult to attract new talent and to expand the organization. The weeds and shrubbery represent the competition an organization faces for the same talent (think "fruit").

It is no mystery that the best way to compete for talent revolves around the concept of "what's in it for me?" from the perspective of an applicant. While this might seem selfish, it realistically is what job seekers want to know when they are applying for and accepting new job opportunities. When Farmer Pyne talks about the consistency needed to keep the weeds from taking over, the same type of consistency needs to exist in several core areas of benefits to the employees.

In speaking with applicants repeatedly throughout the years, it amazes me that one of the greatest "benefits" employees mention the most as related to their jobs revolves around the company culture and environment in which they work. All too often when the word "benefit" comes up, employers quickly jump to thoughts about insurance, a 401(k), paid time off, etc. While these are important aspects, they are not always the only reasons an employee is seeking work or decides to accept an offer of employment. The work environment and workplace culture are the most consistent aspects of a business that exist. The culture is shaped by the rules, which is demonstrated in practice by the core values, and as such, the mission or vision of the company drives the environment.

Understanding what motivates the workers of an organization to be efficient and successful will play an important role in a later chapter, as part of the "trunk" of the Hiring Tree. The benefits of an organization can vary so greatly, that creating a comprehensive list is not only daunting to build, but it may also not be an effective way to help an organization determine what benefits they *should* offer. What should be offered is whatever makes the most sense for the organization, based on the needs of their employees. To be consistent, sometimes you have to do away with or cut back in some areas, and then add others.

One of the greatest examples I have seen for developing benefits based on the needs of employees came from a story shared by Ryan Kohler, CEO of ApplicantPro at the time, which was also a story that I personally watched unfold.

ApplicantPro hires many mothers who are returning to the workforce. Unlike most technology-based companies, eighty percent of the work force at ApplicantPro is female. Some are divorced. Some need extra income to help their spouses. Some are just trying to find an opportunity to work from home to maintain balance in their family life.

Even more daunting is that the circumstances of these workers change all the time. Some remarry, some divorce later on, and some might have a spouse who loses a job, or is injured and is unable to work.

To be consistent, employees are surveyed often to see what needs they have and what may be driving their work ethic. In one of these surveys, conducted several years ago, it was revealed that many of these moms felt bad at the end of the day that their homes were not clean. When they came home from work, they found they were not in the best of moods, and it was difficult for them to concentrate on other aspects of their life due to an inherent need to take care of the cleanliness factor first. When dishes are piled up, the floor is a mess, and the dog hair is scattered all over the place, it can be extremely deflating, especially after a hard day's work.

Ryan decided to act and create a new "benefit" that helped in two ways. It was known as a house-cleaning benefit and was available every month. If certain goals were met by the end of the month, the employee could hire someone to clean their house and be reimbursed up to $100 for the service, which was equivalent to about four hours of house cleaning. For those who did not really need it for the home, the same benefit could be applied to getting a vehicle detailed and cleaned from the messes caused by children.

The reasoning was that when the cleaning is not taken care of immediately, it can pile up, creating an element of stress, anxiety, and a mental breakdown. For the majority of these mothers, it was more than just a "benefit." It was a relief that touched them in a personal way that went beyond work.

I loved hearing this story the most from the founder of one of the cleaning companies hired by ApplicantPro to help with providing the benefit. She used to work for Ryan and was looking for a way to start a business and run something she could be passionate about. ApplicantPro employees have not only become some of her most loyal customers, but because the benefit was offered, it also allowed her to fulfill her dream of starting a business by providing a meaningful service to these wonderful mothers, who work so hard to enhance the customer experience for clients at ApplicantPro throughout the country.

Like ApplicantPro, companies that consistently learn and understand the needs of their employees may also find it much easier to develop and offer additional benefits that are much more meaningful than the traditional benefits that come to mind. What better way to help with company culture than to provide something that truly makes a difference on an individual level!

As you can imagine, employee retention and loyalty create an environment and cohesiveness that trickles into the customer conversations, chats, and emails from employees every day. When we return to the analogy of the apple tree, the feeder roots are strengthened because the weeds and other external factors are not strong enough to prohibit them from helping the tree grow. When the feeder roots are doing their job, the fibrous roots are also strengthened, which then has an immediate impact on the taproot to feed upward toward the growth of the tree. In the winter months, the feeder roots will oftentimes slow down or go dormant until the spring begins again.

The Hiring Tree of an organization can also experience a similar dormancy when a hiring freeze occurs, or there are no needs at the time. It is during this time, when spring comes, that the feeder roots need to pick up where they left off. This is easy to do when the external environment has consistently been maintained. When there is a hiring freeze in an organization, employees can be susceptible to external factors, unless the benefit of working there is solid enough that when hiring starts again, they stay involved and committed to the new employees coming in.

What I loved most about this story is that it was not *only* about trying to find what people wanted or what they liked about the company. It was also about understanding some of the challenges the employees faced in going back to work, and then finding a way to address that difficulty to make it less challenging, and in many cases, overbearing. Ryan's love and appreciation for his employees, acting as the firm taproot for the company, empowered managers with knowledge to support employees in achieving their goal to obtain the benefit.

Similarly, the feeder roots of the tree need obstructions to be removed so that they can be motivated to accomplish their work of feeding the root system to sustain the tree as a whole.

Please remember that insurance, 401(k)s, paid time off, and other benefits that are more well-known still need to be competitive because an organization will have a diverse group of employees, and many will desire these types of benefits. My telling of this story is not meant to make an organization shy away from offering traditional benefits, but I do hope that this story can help companies really think about what they offer, what they should offer, and most importantly, *why* they should offer it. I love to hear stories of unique benefit offerings and always encourage people to share their stories with others to inspire those around them. There are many more good examples of benefits that other companies have offered to personalize their employment experience.

Once the root system has been established, it is time to focus on the trunk of the Hiring Tree, which also consists of three main parts, like the root system of a tree. The base of the trunk system is where my favorite profession comes into play, which is that of the human resource professional. This is such a vital part of an organization in allowing the trunk to shoot upward from the roots to begin creating a beautiful tree, which will eventually bear the right type of fruit.

The role of the human resource professional does not always carry this title. In smaller organizations, this role may be known as the office manager or even an administrative assistant. In mid-level organizations, there might exist a generalist, and as an organization grows, they may even hire a recruiter to focus specifically on these efforts.

Regardless of the job title, all are assigned with the task to help bring in new employees and fill important roles within the organization. In other words, all these roles are expected to plant and grow a Hiring Tree that produces enough fruit to supply the organization with the right employees. In our analogy, as the roots become strong and established, the first stem of the tree pops out of the ground, but this stem is not typically the stem that will establish the core trunk of the tree. What needs to happen then? This process will be described in more detail in the next chapter.

KEEP CALM:
Resource Humans

IN THE PROLOGUE, I mentioned the odds of growing an apple tree that bears edible fruit from a seedling is one in 100,000, making it extremely rare. In fact, most apple trees are purchased from a store when they are already three to five feet in height and are typically well established already. For an apple tree to be successful, it has to receive a graft at the root of the tree once it begins to surface.

Grafting is the art of taking a strong branch from a fruit-bearing tree and grafting it into the root system of the new tree to allow them to blend together and thus establish a core branch that will eventually become the trunk of the tree. The human resources team provides this same balanced blend, from the roots to the trunk that begins the upward reach of an organizational Hiring Tree to bear its most precious fruit, even when that team only consists of one member.

While not always seen this way in some organizations, the human resource team is more powerful in their efforts when they are a part of the executive team, the management team, *and* the employees. This can be challenging for a human resources (HR) team of one, which I see often among smaller organizations. This lonely role is one I have been in myself, which is why in my career, I was always trying to find ways to make things easier, to automate where possible, and to actively involve other members of management to delegate certain responsibilities to those involved in the hiring process.

For those who find themselves in this situation, they are like the farmers, eradicating the gophers, trimming the shrubbery, and managing the weeds; they are the taproot establishing the rules, core values, and mission statement; they take on the role of the fibrous root trying to implement the rules, set the example for the core values and teach the vision of the mission; and finally, they act as the feeder root trying to live the rules and gather the nutrients. The HR professional does them *all* at the same time, which is why they become this grafted branch into the root system to successfully establish a new fruit-bearing tree.

As I have interviewed human resource professionals over the years, almost eight out of ten admitted that they did not start their career in the human resource field, nor did they have any intention of going into such an unknown career. When I earned my degree in finance in December 2004, from Brigham Young University, there were no available degrees that truly focused on the human resource field as a general profession. There were classes here and there that delved into the subject of organizational development, but a true degree in this field did not exist, and if it did, it was not well known.

Many people are involved in the HR process without realizing it. Luckily, there are many options for degrees in this field that exist today, and I always encourage employers who are experiencing growth to consider finding ways to educate those in this role by providing tuition reimbursement. Professional employer organizations (PEOs) are also a great alternative for those who either cannot afford an HR department or are looking to outsource this department until they are big enough to bring this group in-house.

Whether a PEO is used, or someone in-house is eventually placed into this role, it is just like grafting a strong, established branch into the root system of a new apple tree. For those in HR who felt they were thrown into the role, what really happened was they were being grafted in because they were seen as a strong, established branch, and leadership knew they would be a strong contributor that would allow the tree to grow into what was envisioned. This union of branch to roots is such an important part of the Hiring Tree!

My favorite group, which was introduced to me back in 2007, was the Society for Human Resource Management (SHRM). Not only is it one of the most prestigious organizations that promotes sound HR principles, but it also has a certification program that allows organizations to have their employees sit for an exam to test their knowledge in the HR arena. I have been an active member since 2008 in a variety of voluntary roles for SHRM. There has been no better way for me to access an incredible network of professionals to lean on when questions arise, or legal situations present themselves. I have encouraged many organizations throughout the years to have their hiring and organizational development team members join one of their local chapters, in order to develop these skills and relationships, which will continue to help them understand the union of the branch to the roots as mentioned. By allowing their own employees to volunteer and to sit for the exam, an organization can have a team member who is well prepared to manage this important connection.

It is daunting to think about how much this role can have an impact on the Hiring Tree of an organization, because there is so much at stake to ensure the roots feed the rest of the tree in a balanced way. The good news is that it can be accomplished when the HR professional (or the people functioning in this role) know how to delegate, when necessary, know when to push back as appropriate, and know where to provide support in a balanced manner. How is this accomplished? The first step is to really dig into the core of the company to determine whether there is a lack of balance or connection as we have already covered in the root part of the system. Most organizations must start here, because if the foundational part of the system is not addressed first, the rest of the tree cannot flourish. In other words, it is important to make sure the graft is successfully accepted by the root system. An apple tree that does not take to the graft will perish.

The second step is the gathering of information from all of those involved in the hiring process. Just like the roots process the nutrients to send upward into the trunk of the apple tree, those involved in the hiring process need to send the right information upward as the organization begins to reach out to job seekers. While the human resource professional is the typical person doing the gathering, if this type of team member is not available, then an individual or group needs to be assigned the task of being in charge. For smaller organizations that do not have a human resource person or team, the steps are still important to follow, so this assignment cannot be taken lightly. The information gathered will make up the core of the job description and, eventually, the job ad to be used in trying to attract applicants. I am still shocked when I speak with organizations that do not really know what they're looking for, which brings me to another poor example of chaos permeating the process.

I am a big fan of the sport of baseball. When the batter hits the ball, what if it didn't matter which base the runner went to, as long as they touched all four bases in order to score a run? When we introduce more batters as the game progresses, it becomes even more confusing. As more batters are introduced, mass chaos would ensue, because it would be difficult to know which base to run to without a sound understanding of which base the others on the team might be pursuing. The other team would also have difficulty knowing where to throw the ball in order to achieve the three outs needed to give *them* a turn to score runs. To truly understand how confusing this would be, I recommend logging in to Disney+ and searching for the short, as presented by Goofy, called *How to Play Baseball*.

Just like the game of baseball needs rules in order to run the bases in a particular pattern, it is important to understand the pattern of gathering information about roles that needs to be filled within an organization. Unfortunately, too many organizations do a quick search online to find a template for a position they are thinking about filling, and then they give this template to the HR person or the one designated to conduct the search. After this "magical quick-fix" search, they expect applicants to come flowing in, in abundance.

This is where HR might need to be proactive about pushing back, knowing that this magical thought process about hiring is not realistic. There can be resistance when pushing back, but mostly because the one pushing back does not often provide any true guidance as to what they might be seeking. In most cases, this occurs between the manager and the one responsible for finding the new candidate to fill the role. When the communication and grafted connection, as found in the roots, are sound, this is a lot easier to handle. Otherwise, problems ensue due to misunderstanding and miscommunication, leading to an unrealistic expectation of results.

In our analogy, the fibrous roots depend on the feeder roots to gather what is necessary to feed the trunk of the tree. During this gathering process in the organization, conversations are required, not only with those employees in the role currently, or those on the team currently, but also with the manager of the team or the department. For most companies, the HR department is vital in gathering this information, which is the very act of grafting as seen in establishing a new apple tree. For smaller organizations, where departments like this may not always exist, the goal is to help the manager, or individuals involved in the job-posting part of the process, to brainstorm about what is really needed.

If an organization is using job descriptions as their job *ads*, this is the first mistake, and it needs to be corrected quickly. For the rest of this chapter, I am going to focus on what *should* be gathered to allow for optimal success. By following this simple principle of information-gathering, the appropriate type of guidance is allowed, to assist the manager and those involved to accept the graft and establish a solid connection.

Managers

Most arguments and contentious interactions occur during conversations between the manager trying to fill a position and the person posting the job to attract applicants. This is where the push back feels like a game of tug of war, where there really does not seem to be any clear winner.

When the manager tells someone to find a job description and then tweak it a bit and get it posted, this is a true disservice to the person trying to gather more information. This should be a *mutual* conversation, since both are doing their best to fill a much-needed position. On the surface, this does not seem to be that big of an issue, but it is one of the biggest challenges I see, over and over again.

Managers need to understand that this is a team effort. They cannot expect the person posting the job to attract applicants with just a job description (which is probably really boring to read anyway). While a job description is necessary to determine all functions of the role, which in some cases is also a legal responsibility, the reality is that a job description *is not the same* as a job ad. A description is a detailed list of legal jargon defining the role and its functions, but a description in no way entices an applicant to want to apply for the position, which a job ad should be able to accomplish.

The first step is to determine what information should be gathered. One of the best places to start, if possible, is with someone who is currently in the role, the person being replaced, or with those who are currently doing a similar job (or parts of the job).

It is extremely beneficial to start with *who* is in the role and focus on *what* makes them successful. If the role is brand new and there is not really anyone in the role currently, who would be a good match for the position? What attributes would they possess that would lead to that success? What skills would this person bring to the table to guarantee they will flourish? A manager will typically have a good view into who is currently prospering in the position, or an understanding of the right person to fill the position. Defining what success looks like, and determining what this person would be doing that would lead to this success, is such an important part of the information gathering process.

When Farmer Pyne is looking at the trunk of an apple tree, he often will look for areas where the tree might be suffering. This could be due to a disease, a bug, or another outside influence that is causing an issue. He will then find a way to alleviate this pain by providing relief to the tree, so that it can overcome the blight that it is experiencing. This will provide the tree with help and allow the tree proper time to heal and continue to grow. As an example, in the case of bitter pit described earlier, the apples can be sprayed with calcium to heal the tree entirely since this issue is caused by a lack of this much needed nutrient.

When a role is open in an organization, there is typically pain, or needed treatment, to help alleviate the suffering of others in the role, who are taking on too much, or to replace someone who will be leaving. Sometimes, a new department is created due to a new product or service offering. The goal here is to focus on the pain that needs to be remedied.

If the role is *not* filled, what challenges will that bring to the organization? What happens if no one fills the role? This is a critical second step in gathering information, because it helps the manager to truly think about *why* someone is required to fulfill the needs of the position. Like Farmer Pyne with the trunk of the tree, it is necessary to find the source of the pain and determine what will heal that pain within the organization or department.

The third step is what I call the ninety percent rule. While job descriptions oftentimes contain a long list of bullet points, outlining all the possible duties and responsibilities of the role, the focus here is to determine what the new employee will be doing ninety percent of the time. Focusing on the main duties of the position will lead to five to six solid bullet points describing what they are doing *most* of the time. This allows the manager to really home in on what is absolutely necessary, without getting into the little details and menial tasks that aren't necessary. "Other duties as assigned" is great for legal reasons, but it is not sound practice to include this as a bullet point in the job ad itself.

Returning to the analogy of the apple tree, as it begins to grow, after receiving the graft, special care must be taken to prune the tree for the next several years. Farmer Pyne gets really excited to show me new parts of the orchard, where new trees have taken to the graft and are beginning their growth. However, as this growth continues, there are mini branches that start sprouting from the roots that are affectionately called "suckers", and they *must* be removed. This is a constant process for the next several years, as the tree establishes a trunk, to keep the tree from getting out of control.

From the main grafted branch, you may get additional "shoots" that also need to be pruned back to allow for optimal growth of the tree. While it might seem odd to keep cutting the small little branches off, it is a crucial part of the process of developing a trunk with the proper strength to begin growing solid branches. In fact, Farmer Pyne says that the best trees only have a maximum of five to six "shoots" that are kept. All other shoots are cut off to allow for the greatest amount of strength and to focus sending nutrients to these core branches that will bear the fruit. Too many branches will develop into an unruly tree, and none of the branches will be strong enough to bear fruit for a long period of time. Eventually the tree will die if these shoots and suckers are not trimmed away.

For the individual gathering job information from the manager, the ninety percent rule is basically like pruning the details of the job away to focus on the core strength of the role itself, whittling it down to these five to six bullet points previously mentioned. This pruning process also comes into play for the next part of the process as it relates to understanding the requirements and qualifications for the job.

The fourth step is to separate the hard requirements from what I call "preferences" or expectations the manager might have. Often, these two areas are blurred together, causing confusion as to what is absolutely required.

Hard requirements are truly absolute. They are the must-haves of a position, which could be minimal education, minimal work experience, specific certifications, etc. As an example, a nurse without a certification as a registered nurse is not really a nurse. This would be considered a hard requirement in order to work as a nurse for a hospital and requires that the nurse is licensed and certified in the state in which he or she works. It is also important to remember that if the person currently in the role does not have the required education, but the manager is requiring a minimum educational background, this is cause for concern. These types of discrepancies are only revealed when the right questions are asked up front.

Preferences are skills and qualifications that are nice to have, but not absolutely required. They are just expectations the manager might have, although it should be determined up front how realistic these expectations are to the true needs of the position. In many cases, applicants readily admit that they treat preferences like hard requirements, which will deter them from applying. In most cases, listing preferences in the job ad is not the best approach because it may scare away some applicants who are otherwise qualified for the role.

It is important to understand the difference between these two types of requirements, because this can be an element of confusion when writing the job ad, and in my experience, leads to frustration, misunderstanding, and ill feelings on both sides of the information-gathering process.

The final step is to think about the concept most organizations are familiar with. "What's in it for me" is a popular saying that I have often heard, and it comes from the perspective of the job seeker. They will seek answers to questions like:

- Why would someone want to work for this manager specifically?

- What sets this organization apart from other organizations of similar size and/or industry in the area?

- Why does the manager stay with the company and what motivates them in their role each day?

- What makes them passionate about working in their role and leading others?

- What is the approved salary range for the role?

- What is the actual starting range for a new employee, not just the potential salary?

- What are the typical hours that are expected, and are hours flexible or fixed into specifically defined shifts? (Remote work or hybrid work has also become popular since COVID-19, so if there are options to work from home from time to time or all the time, this is important information to know.)

- What benefits are offered for the role, and how would these potentially appeal to the job seeker?

Ultimately, the goal here is to get to the "why" from the perspective of the manager. Have the manager also reveal *why* they think someone would want to work under them as a leader. As mentioned in a previous chapter, if the poor relationship between the manager and the employee is the number one reason for turnover, it is best to gather this information up front because it can become a great selling point for why someone should leave their current situation to come to work under this manager in particular.

Employees

Conversations with employees are just as important as conversations with managers. Sometimes, there is no current employee in the role being filled, so this is not always possible in every scenario, but if it is possible, it will be a similar process as that of speaking to the manager.

The goal here is to gain knowledge from the perspective of the employee that is currently working in the position. I always laugh when I have organizations practice these concepts, only to discover that what the manager says, and what the employee says, are completely different! In fact, if this does *not* happen, I am a little shocked.

The reality is that everyone thinks differently. What motivates one employee may be demotivating for another. While a manager may think their employees do the job for one reason or another, the employees often have a much different perspective, because they are in the role every day. There may be different factors that lead to their passion and desire to do their job daily, and it is such a great experience to dig into this with the employees.

Additional questions, beyond repeating those asked of a manager, might be: What does the employee like or love about their manager, and what are some things they feel could be improved upon?

The great part about this process, too, is that employees feel listened to and appreciated for the role they already play in the organization, and it may excite them to know that more help is on its way, especially if the reason the new role is open is due to their being so successful in their role to begin with.

I think what I have loved most about these activities with organizations over the years is the fact that this process can reveal new training ideas, or allow the creation of additional benefits to offer, as mentioned in the example with Applicant-Pro. Also, it will bring to the surface problems and issues that can now be resolved because they have been revealed.

The reason I relate this process to the pruning of the apple tree is because, over time, trimming away the suckers and the shoots allows the trunk of the tree to become strong, sturdy, and capable of carrying the weight of the branches that will soon bear fruit. Assuming what attracts people to the position versus actually *knowing* what attracts people to the position, is refreshing because it makes a big difference when it is time to write the actual job ad.

Now that the graft has taken root, the suckers have been removed, the shoots have been whittled down, and the nutrients are being fed upward into the leader branch, we can now focus on the next part of the trunk of the Hiring Tree.

JOB DESCRIPTIONS ARE NOT JOB ADS

'LL SAY IT AGAIN, because I cannot emphasize this enough: A job description is *not* a job ad.

In my travels across the country this year, I polled hundreds of employers on their use of job descriptions as their job ads. Over eighty-five percent of the organizations admitted to using some form of the job description to advertise the job. When the Internet was first introduced and the concept of a job board started presenting itself as a viable replacement to newspaper ads, for some reason, the marketing skills learned regarding listing a traditional newspaper ad were lost for a time. It almost feels like those skill sets are considered an ancient language, lost in the sands of a bitter desert storm that buried the rules of listing an ad in a newspaper.

This might be dating myself a little bit, but when I first started my recruiting career, writing an effective and compelling newspaper ad was a skill necessary to be considered a good recruiter! I worked with the marketing director within the organization often to learn these skills as it was part of my training and mentorship within the organization. I am grateful to say that many of these skill sets learned back then are making a strong comeback.

In a newspaper ad, there were certain limitations, so creativity was very important. Those limitations revolved around the concept of "space," which meant that the ad had to be concise, to the point, and attractive enough that the job seeker would reach out to the employer to be considered.

If an organization was not pressed by monetary limitations, they could include images and other eye-catching features with the ad to entice applicants. The classifieds had a job section, where an ad could be placed along with other job ads, and the goal was to have something appealing, in order to move the candidate to action. The call to action was either an in-person visit to the job location to fill out an application, a phone call to the hiring manager or personnel department (HR), or to send a résumé and cover letter in an envelope to the company address. While this might sound prehistoric to many reading this chapter, this was how it was done for hundreds of years. The fact that I used the term "personnel department" is just as revealing.

As the Internet introduced a new way to classify positions (which included images and color), for some reason, the skills needed to write effective newspaper ads was set aside. Those early job boards allowed an ad to be much longer than the traditional newspaper advertising did. The excitement of listing much more information without the limitations of the newspaper listing, led to a quick, but lazy, approach to posting jobs. Despite the lazy actions of the recruiter, the call to action was simple and quick. The résumé and cover letter could now be sent via email instead of "snail mail," as it was affectionately called, and an application could be downloaded, printed, and filled out ahead of time, before coming to the office. Don't laugh, but there still are companies that have a PDF or Word version of their application online for applicants to print off to bring with them to the first interview. For the apple tree huggers out there, this is certainly not an effective way to save those trees!

Recruiting has always been, and will continue to be, marketing. It amazes me that over the years, recruiting has been placed solely in the HR department, and almost appears to be disconnected from marketing altogether, which happened in the early years, as physical newspapers faded away. Even worse, the recruiter began to spend more time just posting the job descriptions and waiting for people to apply.

I admit that it was a lot easier to just "copy and paste," and this process seemed to be a better way to be seen by more people as the ease of the Internet evolved. Unfortunately, ease can lead to a loss of valuable skills and knowledge that are some of the very foundational principles described in this book.

A lot of legal issues also presented themselves, which favored applicants during this era, where it became a requirement in a lot of industries to include the full job description in order to be compliant and ensure the job seeker had all the information up front. I have a personal story that addresses what I call the "Chicken Little syndrome." I made a big mistake early on in my recruiting career that taught me a valuable lesson.

One of the organizations I worked for, prior to the real estate recession, was undergoing an audit, which caused me to reflect and decide that I needed to know more about regulations and laws that could potentially have an impact on my role as a recruiter. This was around the same time I was introduced to the Society for Human Resource Management (SHRM).[7] I was so grateful for the connections within this professional society, which helped me access the resources and information I needed to learn, simplifying the challenges faced during the audit. The knowledge gained helped me to understand why some adjustments needed to be made. I was so excited about what I was mastering, and I immediately decided to implement what I was learning within the organization to change the hiring process.

The sad part about my excitement was that I started acting like Chicken Little, clucking around the office, and talking about the sky falling and how my new game plan to fix the sky was the only option. It turns out that half of what I was learning did not even apply to our industry! In fact, not only did I create *more* work for myself, but I also tried to influence others internally with knowledge that was not even applicable to the business.

While some processes needed modifications, based on some of the information I was learning, the sky was not actually falling, and my Chicken Little attitude and approach was more detrimental than helpful.

Not every law or rule applies in every situation in every industry for every employer. I learned quickly to temper my excitement instead of inciting an unreasonable fear about laws and regulations that did not even apply. Over the years, I have seen a lot of Chicken Littles leave one industry to go work in another industry, thinking that what applied in their previous job was applicable to the new job. There is no reason to assume the sky is falling. As it turns out, it may just be an apple falling from the tree, which is just a natural phenomenon and has no impact on the entire tree.

Similarly to my poor reaction to newfound knowledge, whenever some legal case creates new laws or introduces new ideas or requirements for doing things, it causes disruption that can lead to a variety of outcomes, including what is perceived as falling skies. The bigger issue is when that disruption stirs up the henhouse to create a flock of Chicken Little fanatics, who begin clucking about, expressing opinions about rules that are not applicable in every scenario. I have seen this occur countless times throughout the years.

This same situation happened when the Internet flooded news media channels with the importance of making the full job description available to the job seeker, in order to avoid liability and to set the right expectation for what the job entailed. Hence, the insertion of the famous bullet point already mentioned: "Other duties as assigned." This moment created an influx of job postings into the marketplace that were just the *job descriptions*, causing a shift in mentality among the masses, which led to a loss of valuable skills gained during the era of writing effective newspaper ads.

I have also noticed that, during shifts like this, especially when it is an employer's market (meaning there are fewer jobs than there are applicants) employers tend to assume certain falsehoods. For example, I often hear, "If they *really* want the job, they will fill out the entire application up front" or "we have to have everything up front because it is required by law." These comments are well within the category of falling-sky-type remarks that are not focused on the big picture. Realistically, the full application up front is *not* required of *every* applicant. The full application is only required when applicants have moved to a certain point in the hiring process, because certain qualifications have been met. Only then does it make sense to now require the rest of the application, which is only needed from a select few.

When I begin to hear these types of comments, I really just hear "the sky is falling," and it causes me to cringe a bit. This is when an employer begins to lose sight of the core principles of the hiring process. Their Hiring Tree begins to become malnourished due to carelessly forgetting the simple, consistent acts of taking care of the tree. This is also why when Indeed, and other search engines began to enter the job search marketplace, it suddenly became difficult for traditional job boards to flourish like they had in the past. Companies that noticed this disruption, but also recognized that the core principles of marketing had not changed, they continued to flourish, hiring and growing their organizations despite a job market recession.

The tides then turned the atmosphere into a job *seeker's* market, where there were more jobs than applicants available.

Farmer Pyne knows that when the weather changes, while minor adjustments are made to accommodate, this does not remove the need to continue to nourish and strengthen the tree. For example, if there are rainstorms, he can let up on watering, because the apple trees have sufficient for their needs, but this does not change the need for other nutrients. If there is a drought, then more water and fewer nutrients might be needed due to overexposure to the sun. There must always be a balance, even when external forces cause an imbalance. Just because a new law is introduced that creates an imbalance, it does not mean that everything must shift in that direction. This will disrupt the balance.

The reason I place job ads as part of the trunk of the tree is because job ads should market the position to an applicant by answering the questions they will have, so that, regardless of any disruption, the organization can stay true to the concepts of effective marketing principles. When Farmer Pyne has a bumper crop one year, he does not let up for the following year and stop taking care of his trees. Instead, he continues to nourish his trees, like he has always done, to prepare for the drought that *may* be just around the corner. His high level of consistency creates a well-organized process to nourish and keep the strength and girth his trees have gained over the years.

Consistency in marketing jobs can be related to staying true to these principles of marketing, which will make an organization's Hiring Tree successful in any market. A sound understanding of what the target job seeker will want to know is the most effective way to write a job ad. This is done by recognizing the pain candidates are experiencing in their job search, thus allowing the job ad itself to provide a potential solution through coming to work for the organization.

What's In a Name?

Not all principles of newspaper ad writing are still applicable today, but I want to focus on those core principles of marketing that will help an organization stay consistent, which will continue to provide the proper nourishment to its Hiring Tree.

Back then when the "classifieds" were printed, it would categorize positions into different groups, which were on multiple pages within the paper itself. Those looking for work would pick up the classifieds section of the paper and then search alphabetically for their category of interest and go from there.

When the first job boards entered the Internet scene, they were set up very similarly to newspapers. One would still pick a category to find the list of positions relevant to specific industries or qualifications. It makes sense that it started this way, since this is how people were used to doing a job search.

It is hard to imagine today a world where there were no options to do an actual keyword search to find a job, much less allow the board to guess the word being typed before completing the thought ("smart" technology at its finest). The main job boards started out with categories, not job titles, though it quickly (within a few years) transitioned to job titles, as Internet usage was adopted and gained in popularity due to its ease of use (and lack of black stains on job seekers' fingers).

The first principle to understand involves the job title. Many years ago, as a recruiter, my job title was "senior career development advisor." While this sounded fancy to people who saw it on my business card or started seeing this on my brand-new LinkedIn profile (which was beginning to gain popularity in the business world at the time), it really did not reveal what I actually did. In fact, I see this a lot in organizations, where the name of the role internally does not always help the outside world understand what the role entails. Most people thought that I advised college students on their career paths, based on the word "advisor" in my job title. My role was really just that of a recruiter, or headhunter. My job was to find people who would be a good fit for the organization, present them to hiring managers for review, and expect them to be hired in order to earn the much-needed commission for my efforts.

One of my favorite pastimes is fishing. I have been working in commission-based environments for much of my career, so I have always related to this sport, because the fisherman does not eat unless he catches something. If I do not use the right bait, the fish will ignore my offering, and the day can drag on with nothing to prove how hard I actually worked. When I fish, not only am I moving around to different spots, but I am constantly changing hooks and bait to see what works. The same spot may result in a catch on one day and not on another, even with the same bait. Sometimes the time of day will make a difference. It is constantly changing, which is why most fishermen cannot truly say that there is only one way to do it.

This concept is important to understand because what works one day to attract applicants to apply for a position can change the next day. In fact, when I was recruiting at one time in two different states, the title I used in one state did not work in the other and vice versa because the applicants in that area perceived things differently.

In the state of Philadelphia, we had a sales position open, but if I called it "sales," I would get no bites. I was puzzled because if I used the word "sales" in my job titles in Utah, I would get plenty of applicants.

After a bit of research, I learned that the word "sales" had a bad connotation in Philadelphia, so as soon as I changed the job title to "account executive" (a common term in the area), I suddenly had an influx of applicants for the same position that was called "sales representative" in Utah.

The reason it all starts with the job title is because the job title is the first thing that captures the eyes of a job seeker and needs to be something the applicant may look for. Much like my fish bait, it needs to be enough for the jobseeker to want to, at least, get closer, much like the curious fish, to see what is there.

In a later chapter I am going to talk about search engines and aggregators as one of the branches to the Hiring Tree, which rely heavily on keywords to allow applicants to find you. Another reason the job title is so important is to be *searchable*. Back in the days of newspapers, using symbols and characters was a way to stand out. Today, using symbols or characters get an organization's position blocked or delisted on many job boards, which is why it is important to understand some of the rules that exist out there. Using acronyms, which was also popular in the newspaper days, is also not very helpful. The job title should be clear, concise, relevant, and not written in shorthand.

Content is King

The second principle is to ensure that the content of the job ad contains certain elements. The content of a job ad should be relevant to what a job seeker is looking for. If I were fishing, this would involve researching my target fish to use the right bait to attract them to my lure.

Like the fish, a job seeker wants to understand the simple concept of "What's in it for me?" and will have several questions on their mind as they begin their search. This also means that the content of a job ad should answer the job seeker's potential questions. Too often I see organizations talk about themselves in their job ad, without really thinking about it from the perspective of the person they are seeking to attract. This was also a common practice in the newspaper era to highlight why the organization was the right place to work because of longevity, name recognition, or awards.

While these accolades can be important in the applicant's decision-making process, the reality is that there are enough reviews out there from previous applicants and employees, that this part of the content of an ad should be more about how the job seeker will be able to picture what it would be like to work for the company.

Having worked with millions of applicants over the last seventeen years, I can attest to the fact that there exist three core questions an applicant wants answered before they commit to applying for a job. For the job ad to be effective, the goal of any organization creating an ad should focus on trying to answer these three fundamental questions. These questions should also be very transparent and not appear as an effort to hide or omit information.

The first question to answer for the job seeker is related to the concept of work/life balance. When a job seeker begins the search, they first think about their activities, school, family, and other obligations that may compete with the position. Is the position a full-time or a part-time role? What do the hours look like, and do the hours fit within the timeframe they can commit to? Are there remote options available, or will they need to travel to an office, which introduces a commute to the time allotted?

One of the best ways to answer these questions in a job ad is to let applicants know up front what the schedule looks like. It is also important to understand that the way a *part-time* job seeker thinks is very different from the way a *full-time* job seeker thinks. The same principle applies to a job seeker who wishes to work the mornings, days, evening, or night shift. Since these varying shifts can represent different types of job seekers, ads should be written entirely differently for varying shifts.

The most common mistake I see in organizations today is to post one ad for all shifts, which also encompasses part-time or full-time time roles. This will limit visibility, because the job seeker is typically looking for something specific to fit their schedule, which is why it is much more effective to market these roles as different ads altogether.

Another danger here is to simplify by copying and pasting the same ad, word for word, for each different role. As mentioned previously, simplification has led to a lackadaisical way to post job ads for a lot of companies, especially organizations that do not have the name recognition of the bigger companies, which permeate the job boards.

To truly stand out, it is important to use a variety of ads that target the job seeker based on what they seek. This is why a previous chapter focused on finding out what current employees like about the role in which they work. Why was full-time or part-time attractive to them? What is it about the manager they enjoy the most? These are some of several elements that can be placed in the job ad to better attract someone to the role who may be looking to escape the situation they are currently in, especially because their current position may not fit their work/life balance already.

The second question to answer for the job seeker is the most taboo topic in the job market today, and has been for a long time. It revolves around the subject of listing salary or pay information. I often hear from an organization that they do not list pay because the manager or the executive team is against it. When asked why, the most common answers are "We don't want the competition to know what we pay," or "We don't want to scare people away because we may offer something lower than they expect or can get elsewhere."

These false notions often have no credibility or proof associated with them, making them sound very similar to the "sky is falling" concept I shared earlier. The chapter on search engines will make this much clearer from this perspective, but perhaps more important is the fact that nine out of ten applicants I have surveyed in the last year will readily admit that, if pay is not listed, they simply do not click on the ad. In fact, seven out of ten applicants will also admit that, when an organization does not list pay, they feel like the company may be hiding something, which leads them to believe that there is an element of dishonesty already present. This is not a great way to begin a working relationship.

When someone meets someone else for the first time, and it feels like the other person is hiding things, or omitting certain facts on purpose, how much time will be dedicated to actually developing a relationship? Information is so readily available today that omitting pay and salary information decreases credibility for the organization right off the bat. This leads to a loss of many qualified applicants, who could have filled the role had the company been transparent about what was being offered to begin with.

Demonstrating a shy attitude about listing pay also indicates that there may be other underlying issues. If an organization cannot feel confident about what they offer, then this is worth addressing. What is being offered should be competitive when *coupled with* everything else an organization provides. There needs to be a high level of passion and excitement that revolves around the offering, an energy that was collected during the discussion with employees and managers.

That said, when listing pay, a *range* is best, but caution needs to be taken so as not to put in a range that is not realistic, or that is too far from what is reasonable. The best rule of thumb is to only include a pay range where an organization is willing to *start* the applicant. For example, a range of $50,000 to $75,000 is a big gap. If, in this example, an organization knows they are only willing to start someone for up to $55,000, then the listed range in the job ad of $50,000 to $55,000 is sufficient, realistic, and honest. If other bonuses, commission, or other options for more are available, it never hurts to address this separately, within the body of the ad, *after* listing the main pay range. I have also seen "starting at" with the minimum wage the company is willing to offer.

The third and final question to answer for the job seeker is that of benefits offered. As mentioned previously in the gathering stage of information, benefits are not just about the health, dental, 401(k), and other types of common benefits (in part because they may not even be offered). This is where demonstrating how effective the organization can be in helping the applicant find relief from their current state of pain will make all the difference.

Over the years, I have often invited clients to read the reviews of their competitors as it relates to working for them. Some of these reviews can be very revealing. I had a manufacturing client once find out that the reason people were recently leaving their competitor was due to a new schedule that forced many employees to work weekends and evening shifts, something that had not been required before. Since my client had separate employees working those shifts, they rewrote the benefits section of the day shift job ad to include how important it was to be able to work during the day and be with their families at night and on the weekends.

The schedule someone works is often seen as a benefit, too, and when this company targeted their job ads to focus on the pains, as described in these negative reviews, they began to attract many competitor employees to their positions. These newly hired team members then helped the organization win a new contract, which almost doubled their revenue for that division within four months! The new employees were so excited to leave the state of pain they were in working shifts they did not want to work. The job ads targeted this pain *and* outlined a solution to the negative impact of what they were experiencing, which made all the difference in the company's ability to attract more applicants for their jobs.

I love this example because finding creative ways to help the job seeker understand why they should make a move from where they are currently makes for a great argument, propelling the job seeker to act, by sending their information to the employer.

There are ways to modify job ads to make it about the candidate and not about the company. As an example, instead of talking about their most recent award, an organization can write about the fact that, because of their employees and the types of people who work for them, it led to the award being given, granting a fulfilling experience for new employees who choose to apply and potentially work for them. I often will tell my clients their goal should be to make an applicant read a job ad and make any of these statements: "That sounds like me!" or "This sounds like a great place to work!" or "I can't wait until they call!" These kinds of statements affirm that it is an *effective* job ad.

Applicants have a pain they are looking to alleviate, and the job ad should be written in such a way as to make the applicant commit to submitting a résumé or application. In marketing, this is known as a "call to action," which is the ultimate goal of every effective job ad.

Too Long or Too Short?

The third principle revolves around the length of an ad. There are just a few more elements of effective job ads to cover before we jump to the last part of the trunk of the Hiring Tree in the next chapter.

A job ad should not be too long or too short. If it is too short, it can come across like common job ad fraud, where scam artists post really short ads to try to quickly attract a candidate to submit information. Plus, it may not be rich enough in content to cause the reader to continue to read. The goal is to have a job ad that does not appear to be a scam. It needs to appear that time was actually spent in its creation.

If the ad is too long, candidates can lose interest and move on, especially when the content itself does not help answer the job seeker's questions. Ideally, job ads should be between two hundred to five hundred words, but again, the ad size is not as important as meaningful content, as previously mentioned.

An ad should capture the attention of the job seeker, similar to the newspaper ads of days past. Over the years, ads that fall within these parameters are not only effective at attracting applicants, but they also make it very easy to effectively follow the "1 to 2 percent rule" mentioned in a later chapter as it relates to the use of target keywords within the body of the ad itself.

The principle of pruning an apple tree applies to the content of a job ad as well. An ad should not list *every* possible scenario an employee may experience in the role with a long list of bullet points and possibilities, or those "duties as assigned" options. Sticking to the core qualifications of a role, clearly defined preferences, and three to five bullet points describing what an employee will be doing 90 percent of the time, is perfect. This makes it a lot easier to fall within the parameters of two hundred to five hundred words. Simplicity, transparency, and being specific about the roles are the best way to create an effective ad.

Much like the trunk of an apple tree that will send nutrients into the branches to produce the blossoms that become fruit, job ads are a powerful anchor to effectively market the role to the branches where applicants are ready to blossom into the fruit needed to fill those open requisitions. This is the most powerful way to get the right message out there, regardless of the source used to attract applicants.

Finally, keep in mind that job advertising is a moving target. Similar to when I am fishing, where I move spots or change my bait, job ads sometimes need to be changed up a bit to attract people at different times or locations. In fact, the way the ad is written may appeal to one group of applicants, whereas a different ad may appeal to another group. This is a great way to maintain diversity in the applicants you attract, too, because real diversity exists all around us in every type of person.

A common bad practice I see is to keep using the same job ads that have always been used. When done this way, it will continue to attract the same people you have always attracted in the past, which may not be what you are targeting. There is also a concept in marketing called "ad fatigue," where seeing the same message over and over may lead to job seekers ignoring the ad altogether. Just like the newspaper ads of old, the goal is to attract the *right* people to the ad, not just anyone. In our analogy of the apple tree, we want it to bear fruit, but not all fruit is good for keeping and taking to the markets.

While the elements discussed in this chapter are sound, the way a job ad is written can make all the difference, and it may need to be changed from time to time. Just like my manufacturing client who changed their ads to address what was happening nearby at a local competitor. Sometimes, changing things to fit the environment in the moment is crucial to success. What will not change is the importance of providing *answers* to the questions applicants are asking when they are looking for work, even when those questions may adjust from time to time. They want to know what's in it for them, why they should work for the company they are applying for, and how it will resolve the bad situation they are looking to leave. Much like an apple tree will always need certain vitamins and nutrients to bear the best type of fruit, the information in job ads should be consistent and specific to the type of applicants a company seeks to attract, thus providing the nutrients needed.

The next chapter will focus on the final section of the trunk, which has evolved heavily since the days of newspaper ads. Once the applicant is attracted to the job ad, it would be a shame to lose them while they are completing the application. It is kind of like hooking the fish, attempting to lift it up into the net, and then watching it drop back into the water due to a weak, broken fishline.

No one wants to share a big fish story about the "one that got away."

CRABAPPLE-CATION
PROCESS

CRABAPPLES typically get a bad rap because the term "cra-bapple" is often used to describe someone who is unpleasant to be around or someone who tends to act crabby. These varieties of apples are typically much smaller in size than normal apples, and they tend to be very sour, and sometimes very bitter, making them inedible for eating right off the tree. However, they do serve a purpose in making jellies, jams, cider, and other preserves, and they are very effective at helping with pollination, because they blossom before many of the normal apple trees and attract the bees early on. They flower really well, too, so the visual appeal they provide can be inspiring during the spring, when the trees begin to blossom, causing young couples to flock to the orchard for those perfect wedding photos. Often, sugar is added to these types of apples, covering the sour or bitter taste, to make them more appealing to the general populace.

In continuing the analogy of the Hiring Tree, the last part of the trunk has to do with the application process a job seeker must go through to be considered for employment. This is one of the bitterest of experiences for the applicant when done incorrectly, even if the employer tries to sweeten it up with flowery words and promises. I jokingly call it the "crabapple-cation" process, and it has amazed me over the years to see how often employers seem to make the application process extremely difficult.

While job ads are one of the first impressions an applicant will have with an organization, the application process itself is their second impression. It is extremely important to consider what kind of impression the organization wishes to make at this stage.

Historically, as job ads moved from newspapers to the Internet, applicants had the opportunity to send a résumé, cover letter, or other details, via email or fax. As this continued to evolve, job boards began offering employers the ability to collect résumés and information online, where employers could review and manage applicants in a better way, which led to the creation of applicant tracking systems, or ATS for short.

These systems gave employers the opportunity to accept full applications, together with résumés, online, relieving an employer of the burden of tracking candidates in a variety of different places such as email, the job boards, faxes, Excel spreadsheets, and other accounts. However, the introduction of tracking systems also introduced a unique challenge to the user experience for applicants who expressed interest in applying for a job. Just like filling out paper applications became a tedious process for job seekers, it was amplified as online systems began to enter the market. While finding companies to apply to became easier, the challenge of filling out an online application was just as strenuous to the job seeker as the paper version, because applicants were spending more time filling the same information out repeatedly. Instead of becoming easier for the candidate, this made it more difficult for the job seeker to commit to the time needed to submit applications online, resulting in many abandoning the process. Employers may not have noticed this at first because these types of systems entered the scene during an *employer's* market, where there were more applicants than jobs available.

As tracking system companies noticed this trend of complaints from job seekers, the concept of "résumé parsing" was introduced to simplify things for the applicant. Résumé parsing is basically the ability for an online form to parse information from the résumé into the fields on the application, pre-filling in many of the sections, to save the applicant time by avoiding some of the manual data entry. While this helped, many employers decided that they still wanted a full application, which contains a lot of fields that are not found on a résumé, so the parsing only partially helped.

Applicant tracking systems then began to partner with some of the major job boards in order to parse information from the candidate profiles from that job board into the application on the ATS, which helped a little more, but still not enough. This concept is known as "profile parsing," which is much more popular today.

Due to legal issues, many employers wanted so much information up front that, in many cases, online applications continued to get longer. With the introduction of electronic signature laws, it now became necessary for applicants to create an account with the tracking system in order to stay compliant and collect the e-signature.[8] Much like inclement weather conditions in an apple orchard that can disrupt the growth of the trees, these legal issues were an example of yet another disruption to the balance and simplicity that online systems were trying to create.

Over the past decade, applicant tracking software companies have been placed in the middle of a tug of war between the job boards trying to simplify the application process for the job seekers, and the employers trying to stay compliant and collect as much information as possible to simplify things on their end. Therefore, software companies often struggle to understand how to please both, which is why I have seen many of these companies go out of business over the years.

Most employers use tracking systems like ApplicantPro to help with applicant management, which I highly recommend, but not all tracking systems help the employer to *attract* applicants. In fact, many systems will scare applicants away, causing an even greater disruption to the hiring process.

For an apple tree, as the trunk begins to grow its core branches, it is vital to be able to send the right amount of nutrients to allow the branches to bear fruit. Too many nutrients can hurt the tree, even though nutrients are required. The application process is this vital connection from the branches to the trunk of the tree. If the information on the application itself represents the nutrients needed by an apple tree, the right amount of nutrients should be required, but not so much so as to overwhelm the bearing of the fruit.

For small organizations, an applicant tracking system is a great way to manage applicants from a variety of sources all at once, because it acts as a hub for all sources, including the company website and employee referrals. Small employers are often tempted to use multiple job boards, creating multiple accounts and managing applicants from the boards themselves. However, this makes it very difficult to manage applicants from a variety of sources all at once, because the hiring manager needs to log in on multiple boards. Once information is sent to others in the hiring process, there is little to no visibility as to what happens from that point, adding to the difficulty of managing the candidates that apply.

When the process is cumbersome to the employer, it can create an inefficiency that creates a bad experience for the applicant (like a lack of nutrients provided to create the fruit). While considering the options here, there are three extremely important elements that *must* exist in the applicant tracking system an organization decides to use.

The first element is to have the proper connections to the major job boards. This includes places like Indeed/Glassdoor, ZipRecruiter, LinkedIn, CareerBuilder, Monster, Refer.io, and other job boards where a full integration is *possible*. Many tracking systems function via a redirect only for these major job boards. A redirect means that when the applicant finds an ad on a job board, and then the candidate clicks "apply", they are *redirected* to the applicant tracking system, or the website, to fill out the application. This is an important concept to understand because, while many systems will tout the fact that they can push jobs to these major boards, they often fail to talk about the actual process and omit whether a full integration actually exists. If the tracking system is *only* a redirect, statistics that we tracked at ApplicantPro years ago, show that almost seven out of ten applicants will abandon the process <u>during</u> the redirect. This means that as soon as they are redirected, they will give up, causing the employer to lose out on potential applicants that would have applied had it been easier to do so. The number one reason for this abandonment is because, when the applicants land on the page and must search again, or fill out the application from scratch, they revert to other employers that allow an easier process.

Many of the major boards mentioned earlier have "easy apply" or "quick apply" options available, where the profile information of the applicant is automatically sent to the tracking system and the redirect never happens. In fact, this full integration will also display job-specific screening questions, and other fillable fields from the application, that the applicant can fill out right away, making it a simple three-to five-minute process. If the tracking system being used does not allow for some of these easy/quick-apply options, then it is either time to pressure the tracking system company to build these integrations or to look for a different vendor.

I cannot emphasize enough how important this process of simplification has become, especially with the introduction of mobile-friendliness several years ago. Much like résumé parsing, these easy/quick-apply options will parse profile details and even send the résumé over to the ATS, making it an ideal option for the applicant, which produces more applicant flow. I remember when using a mobile device was considered clunky and difficult, so to think about applying for a job from a cell phone was unheard of! In dealing with applicant flow on a daily basis in my current role, over 80 percent of applicants are applying from a mobile device now, which makes the easy/quick-apply features that much more attractive to the job seeker. Being mobile-friendly is very much part of this quick-apply option and is a must-have as part of the tracking system.

The second element is the length of the application. Simplification is always best, and the best type of process I have seen goes back to the newspaper days. Back in those days, most job seekers were prompted by the classified ad to send a résumé, cover letter, and other basic contact details to the employer. From there, the employer would review the information and then decide whether it made sense to move the candidate to the next stage of the process and have them come in for an interview. If there was additional paperwork, or other forms required, the applicant would fill this out at the time of the interview. In other words, there were two basic steps to the process: first, have the applicant send basic information for consideration, and then provide more information if, and only if, they were moved to the next step of the hiring process.

For online options today, the two-stage application process has made a very strong comeback. Collecting the basic details from the quick-apply functions of the job boards up front is known as the first stage. This is collected of *all* applicants who want to be considered for employment. Once a review has taken place by the employer, applicants are then invited to fill out the rest of the application as required by that specific organization. This can be done after a phone screen, after a face-to-face interview, or even at the point of hire, making an offer contingent upon the applicant completing the rest of the full application.

I often equate this part of the process to dating apps. While I have never used an app for dating, I am intrigued by the description of the process, because it relates to the job application process. In a lot of dating apps, it is a swipe left or a swipe right. If there is a match by swiping right, a connection is made, and the two parties can begin their communication with one another if desired. Sometimes that initial phone screen eliminates one or the other and the process stops. Sound familiar?

In the job application process, it is very similar. This first stage is where the swiping occurs, where the applicant expresses interest in the role. In a dating app, it is just pictures and the basic profile that create the call to action to "swipe," and while it sounds a little superficial, the initial attraction has to exist up front in order for the potential relationship to be successful later down the road as connections are made.

When an applicant can submit some of these basic details at the first stage of the process after seeing the job ad (think "dating profile"), the employer is able to convert visitors into actual applicants (swipes), thus increasing the number of applicants that come through (we have a match!).

Often I hear from employers, especially those under heavy legal compliance, that they have to have the full application up front. The reality is that this is not the case and is one of those moments of playing the role of Chicken Little. Part of the legal definition of a viable Internet applicant requires that the candidate be "considered" for a particular position and meets the "basic qualifications." While the applicant has done their swipe by sending over their initial information in this two-stage process, the employer still must do their own swipe for them to be considered an actual applicant as defined by law. This means that a second stage of the application process is completely legal and can be used to comply with the legal definition of an "applicant" that may come up during an audit in reference to record-keeping requirements.

The key here is to ensure that there is not a disparate impact[9] in the actual process when the employer makes their swipe. I have been through enough audits with clients over the years, that it is refreshing to know that this two-stage process is perfectly legal and falls within the parameters of current legal definitions. Don't make the same mistake I used to make by playing the role of Chicken Little as part of the application process. It is not a fun place to be and may be scaring certain qualified applicants away, which, in and of itself, might be considered its own disparate impact!

Luckily, most companies are not heavily regulated, so this will only apply to certain organizations. However, the ability to qualify applicants is a critical part of the process, which can be automated, making the use of an applicant tracking system that much more attractive, even to small employers.

With the thought of qualifying an applicant in mind, this leads to the final element that must be part of the applicant tracking system used by an organization. This revolves around the use of what many will call "knock-out questions." I have also heard the terms "screening questions" or "job-specific questions."

The purpose behind these types of questions is to automatically disqualify applicants who do not meet certain criteria (such as level of education, years of experience, certifications, etc.). They focus specifically on the hard requirements gathered as part of the root system outlined in a previous chapter. A solid tracking system will not only have this option, but these questions will also be fully part of the first stage of the process, becoming a critical piece of the easy/quick-apply functions.

For those who are heavily compliant, this absolutely *must* be part of the first stage. The most effective use of job-specific screening questions is to solely make them about the hard requirements. Similar to the pruning rule we have mentioned before, as it relates to an apple tree, ideally, there should never be more than ten of these knock-out questions at this initial stage. In practice, I have found that five to seven questions are best and should *never* be fill-in-the-blank questions. Ideally, job questions should only be yes/no, or the even-more-popular drop-down, menu-type questions or checklists, because of the impact they have on preferences desired by the manager. In other words, like swiping in a dating app, they should be quick and easy, since many applicants today are applying from a mobile device anyway. There is no better way to increase the number of applications coming through at the onset of the process than keeping job questions simple and straightforward.

A dating app does not ask the other person to share his or her entire life story up front in order to be considered, so why would an employer ask for the entire life story of an applicant as part of the first stage of the application process? It is much more logical to have a few knock-out questions to determine initial qualifications, allowing the employer to pay a bit more attention to the applicant's record and résumé. This also makes it simpler for the hiring manager, so they are not wasting countless hours sifting through applicants who are obviously not qualified for the role.

There is one additional bonus element to consider that is also part of the job questions that many tracking systems might have. It revolves around those "preferences," as defined by the managers during the gathering stage of information, in the root phase of the Hiring Tree.

Not only can job-specific screening questions be added,

with certain answers to disqualify the job seeker, but some of the answers can also be scored or ranked to further filter applications more qualified than others based on manager preferences. For example, if the role does not require a certain level of experience, but the manager *prefers* five years of experience, as opposed to only three years, this is where scoring is extremely beneficial. By providing a list the applicant can choose from and scoring the answer of "five years" higher than the answer of "three years," this creates a way for the hiring manager or team to not only disqualify applicants, but to also give them a score that can then be filtered accordingly.

Back in the days of newspaper ads, this was one of the most challenging parts of the process, because hiring managers had to spend countless hours sifting through a stack of résumés to determine initial qualifications. Technology has made this much easier to handle by automating the process in powerful ways. If an applicant tracking system does not allow this option to screen applicants automatically, the employer should consider different options that are more viable in the two-stage process, since it is the most powerful way to get more applications (even if a lot of them are just the leaves on the tree that can now be sifted).

A word of caution to mention here is a common term used in the world of human resources known as an "all-in-one solution." The concept of an all-in-one solution is a software platform that does it all: payroll, timekeeping, onboarding, off boarding, employee tracking and management, applicant tracking, etc. However, many of the major platforms that exist out there aren't good at *everything*, since they typically started out within one area and became experts in that area. In fact, many of these systems, having started out as a leader in one area such as payroll, then bought out other companies in the other areas, or later built something to be able to check the box that they offer an "all-in-one solution." Not only does it seem like duct tape was used to piece the programs together, but many HR professionals will be the first to tell you that it also feels like the duct tape is *barely* holding them together.

Sometimes the best programs are those that specialize in a core area, such as applicant tracking, and then connect to other programs that are good in other areas. Technology is such that there are easy ways to piece things together without it feeling or looking like they were duct taped. So careful research should be done to truly understand what is meant by an "all-in-one solution" when it is pitched.

While I might sound a little biased on this topic, over the years I have seen a lot of organizations return to the ApplicantPro platform because the all-in-one solution just didn't perform as they had hoped. In other words, the apple looked great on the outside because it was shiny, but upon taking a bite, it was a mushy mess, with little to no flavor. What is interesting about this concept is that big stores coat apples in wax and flash freeze them, and hold them in cold storage for up to six months or more. That is why they look shiny on the outside but are mushy on the inside. By the time they are pulled from the freezer and placed on the shelves for purchase, they are no longer as fresh as when they were initially picked. If you have ever bitten into an apple right off the tree, you will immediately notice the crispiness of the apple as it breaks from the core.

Now that the graft has been established at the base of the trunk, attractive job ads have been created to move candidates to action, and an easy application process has been implemented with effective filters in place, it is now time to address the first branch of the Hiring Tree, which is the most important branch of the entire tree. Without this branch, and the strength it provides to the entire tree, the tree will rot from the inside and eventually become a part of the smoldering pile at the end of the season. I have seen organizations rise and fall due to the impact of this branch alone.

THE LEADER BRANCH:
Empowering Employees to Share

W HEN THE GRAFT OF AN APPLE TREE is accepted by the root system in the beginning stages of its life, for the next several years of growth, there is one solid branch that will strengthen as it moves upward. This branch is known as the "leader branch." The base of this branch becomes the solid foundation that will eventually make up the trunk of the tree, which connects to both the roots and the branches.

It is from this leader branch that the other five or six core branches will emerge, constituting the main branches of the tree for the rest of its life. As the shoots and suckers are snipped away over the next few years, the leader branch will absorb most of the initial nutrients to sustain and strengthen the whole tree, especially as it begins to create the main branches that will bear most of its fruit. During these delicate years, this leader branch will produce some of the first fruit and will also be a good indicator of how fruitful the tree is going to be as it matures.

For an organization's Hiring Tree, the leader branch is the company's employee referral program. Employee referrals have been, and will always be, the strongest, most fruitful of all the branches, which is why this branch needs the greatest amount of care and attention.

The challenge posed by this particular branch is that employee referrals do not always produce fruit. Sometimes they bear only leaves, or sometimes they bear a *type* of fruit, but the kind of fruit that is not really good enough to take to the market.

One of the biggest mistakes I have seen over the years is that a company will interview *every* employee referral, regardless of qualifications or skill sets, which is a poor way to nourish this particular branch. This is why I often hear hiring managers or HR say that they are not fans of employee referrals. The reason they experience this is because they are actually hiring the leaves or crabapples, which is not the right approach to this branch.

Those conducting the interviews will often feel obligated to interview, or worse, hire these referrals, because of what the hiring manager thinks they represent. If an employee referral program is to succeed and provide the necessary base of the entire tree, this branch must be strengthened and nourished correctly. Since this program will also have an impact on all other branches, getting it right is of utmost importance. Below, I'll share the best steps to ensure a successful program.

Several years ago, I was given a book called *Good to Great* by Jim Collins that introduced a unique concept in business called a "flywheel." The flywheel term originates in the world of mechanics, where a heavy circular wheel takes a lot of effort and force up front to gain momentum, but once in motion at high speed, the flywheel runs by itself with little to no effort. An effective employee referral program is much like this concept.

Just like the leader branch of an apple tree starts out small and thin, as it gains in strength and girth, it becomes the trunk of the tree, sustaining the tree for the rest of its life, without using up most of the nutrients, because it can now focus on sending most of the nutrients to the other branches.

The rest of this chapter will focus on the flywheel concept of an employee referral program to give the reader a basic guide to begin the process. This process may take a considerable amount of effort up front, but once momentum is established, like with the motion of a mechanical wheel, the system itself can run effortlessly with small, consistent steps going forward.

Employee referral program
with gratitude at the heart

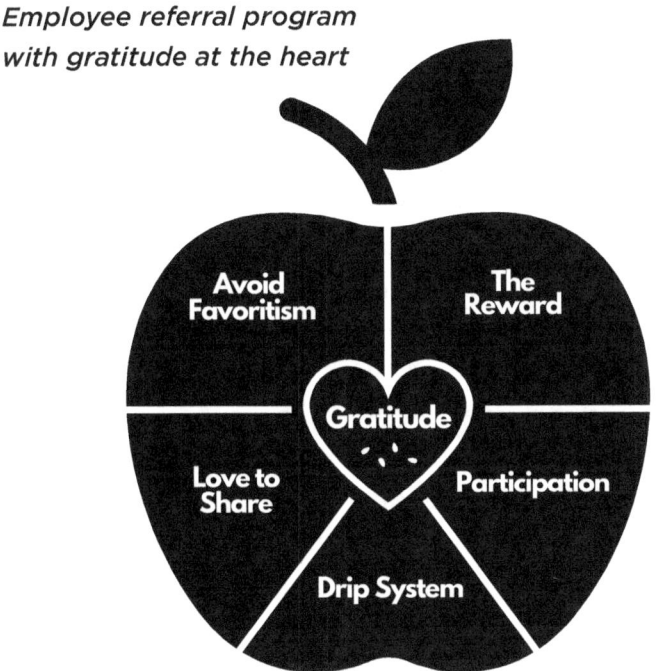

STEP ONE: The Reward

When I started my recruiting career, like many recruiters, my pay structure was based on my ability to do my job effectively. This meant that, as I made an effort to find qualified applicants and presented them to managers, the goal was not only to produce a new hire, but to also introduce someone who had enough longevity to stay with the organization for the long term.

The two sides of this equation meant that my commission and reward were given to me much later in the process, such as after the ninety-day probationary period, the six-month review, or the annual checkup of the new hire. The longer someone stayed, the more I would make, because what I brought to the table made an impact for a long period of time.

Unfortunately, this payout practice is also applied to many employee referral programs today and is not the best approach. The question that must be asked by the organization is this: Is an employee a recruiter? If the answer is no, then why would the company reward the employee like they would a recruiter?

Most employee referral programs do just that. The bonus is given to the referring employee after the new (referred) employee starts and has been there for a certain period of time, just like it is with a recruiter or a staffing agency.

Interviewing every employee referral regardless of skill or experience, even feeds this type of approach, because it gives the employee a false sense of hope, since the referral is moving on to the next step. While there appears to be no risk to the employer from a monetary perspective, since the reward is given much later in the process, there is more at risk than they might realize. Part of the reason for this type of reward system may stem from the fact that the recruiter often developed and created the employee referral program to begin with, so they thought rewarding the employee like *they* were rewarded was the best way to approach the program. While this might be great for the sales-oriented recruiter of the organization, not everyone is motivated by the same approach, especially the majority of employees.

In conversations with employees from hundreds of organizations over the years, they shared with me several reasons why they were reluctant to participate in an employee referral program. One of the top reasons is because the reward is given much later, so it doesn't seem feasible to participate. Due to inefficiencies that may exist in an organization, there is also a danger present where the employer may forget to give out the reward, leading to additional frustrations from the employee.

Instead of treating an employee like a recruiter, an employee should be rewarded based on their role in the process, which is that of sharing and spreading the word. They should be recognized for their role as an emissary of the organization, even if it is just a recognition of the effort made. As soon as the employee has discussed the company with others, to share jobs that are actively open, their role as a company ambassador begins to produce the fruit of new applicants. Even when those people do not *apply* for a job, the employee has now placed a seed in the mind and heart of another individual, which leaves a good impression of the organization that could lead to an applicant later, or possibly new business.

The best types of reward systems I have seen include immediate rewards when a referral is hired, even if it is a smaller amount than what had been paid in the past. I have seen tiered structures as well, where an immediate reward is given up front, and then additional rewards at other intervals. The immediate reward is the *most well received*, because it is a great way to say, "Thank you for sharing the jobs, which is what we asked you to do." Again, the goal here is to thank the employee for simply sharing the jobs with their network, not for being a recruiter for the organization. Rewarding employees because they share is the best way for the organization to show they care about those efforts. If an employer waits sixty days or more after the hire, they have already lost some of the momentum that could have been achieved with an immediate reward.

STEP TWO: Contests for Maximum Participation

Contests that allow rewards for locations, teams, or other circles found within the organization are a great way to encourage as many people to participate as possible. Rewards can include prizes, gift cards, a parking spot, an extra day off, a free lunch, company vehicle privileges, group BBQ, etc.

The culture of the company may help define the best types of rewards to be given. The larger the organization, the greater the total number of rewards for contests should be. For example, rather than one grand prize, create rewards for the top three, top ten, or top twenty-five (it can vary based on the size of an organization), because the odds of getting a reward for "playing the game" are much higher, thus increasing participation in the program.

Keeping rewards small, but having *many* rewards, is a great way to increase the odds, leading to an increase in the number of employees who will join in on the action. In fact, in tracking the use of contests with many clients for the past two years alone, I have seen an increase in employee participation by 46 percent on average, and in many cases the increase in number of referrals per employee reaches almost 300 percent. This has worked in a variety of industries with a variety of employer sizes, ranging from twenty-five employees to upwards of ten thousand. Even a pandemic did not seem to slow down participation or desire for employees to become involved when they felt the odds of winning were much higher with little prizes instead of one grand prize.

STEP THREE: Drip System

Farmer Pyne has a "drip system" to water his trees, which includes a connection of pipes scattered throughout the farm in a particular pattern, which constantly drips water to quench the thirst of his fruit trees. The best part about this type of system is that it is consistent, providing a steady flow of water to help with their growth without drowning the trees.

When it comes to a solid employee referral program, a drip system of messaging works best. Consistent messaging is the most effective, as long as it is not overbearing or too often. This messaging should act as a good reminder of why participating is beneficial to the employee and the company.

As an organization, we have tested a variety of messaging options with thousands of companies. Monthly reminders are often too far apart, making the program forgettable. A weekly newsletter or email seems to work best, so employees are reminded to participate by sharing with friends, neighbors, groups, old coworkers, other colleagues, and people they may come in contact with throughout the week. Plus, if there are new positions posted on a weekly basis, this is very effective, because there is something new and fresh every week.

Automating these messages can be very effective, just like Farmer Pyne automates his watering to turn off and on based on certain schedules. When it rains, he adjusts the schedule, because the trees do not need the extra water. An organization that may not be hiring at the time can spread out the messaging to biweekly or monthly until new roles open up, changing it back to the weekly reminders.

STEP FOUR: Share the Love, and Love to Share

Sometimes the reluctance of an employee to share is due to a feeling of being coerced into participating to get more people to join the organization, making it feel more like a multi-level marketing company instead of an effort to grow the organization in a natural way. In case this is a new concept to the reader, a multi-level marketing (MLM) company is often built based on a downline of people who join the organization underneath someone else. The goal is to find anyone willing to join underneath the main person, so that a select few people at the top of the pyramid make a lot of money based on the efforts of everyone below them.

Most people in these organizations feel obligated to try and get every family member or colleague to join underneath them in hopes of getting wealthy very quickly. The drive and motivation to refer people is fueled by selfish intentions rather than a genuine desire to help those recruited.

The strongest type of referral program is one where sharing jobs feels much more natural, like the taste of a fresh, crisp apple picked from the tree. When someone works for a great manager, a great team, or a great company, it is natural to want to share the positive experience with others they encounter.

Just in case the employee knows, or meets someone, looking for an opportunity to improve their career path in some way, the goal here is to create a program that is simple, straightforward, and readily available so the employee can share when the moment arrives. In other words, an innate desire has grown within the employee that has become strong enough to *want* to share the open position, because working with the organization has created an impact on a personal level, resulting in the employee experiencing a sense of growth and belonging.

Sharing jobs must be easy *and* simple and must give an employee the surety that they will get credit for what they are sharing. Technology makes this process very simple by creating specific links that work best when they automatically insert the employee's name as the referral source, regardless of where the employee chooses to share the link. Many tracking systems have the capability to do this within the system itself, thus pushing employee referrals directly into the system for review by hiring managers. Although I did not mention this in the previous chapter as an ultimate requirement in the selection of a tracking system, this is such an essential part of an organizational Hiring Tree, because as the leader branch, small companies will find new employees as they begin their growth, and bigger employers will continue their steady growth through employee referrals as they mature.

When employees feel like they are getting credit for sharing and the ability to share is simple, this will create a team of ambassadors for the organization. There is nothing more powerful than an employee who shares a position, because they will commonly include in their post a reason *why* they love to work for the organization, which serves as a powerful witness to what the company offers, what the company represents, and why the potential job seeker should submit their information for consideration.

STEP FIVE: Avoid Playing Favorites

Another danger that can impact an employee referral program is the concept of nepotism or favoritism. This is why it is so important to stick to the core qualifications for the role and choose to interview only those referrals who are *actually* qualified to move forward in the hiring process.

For those organizations that are under a lot of compliance, this only helps them stay compliant, since nepotism and favoritism can lead to outright discrimination or a disparate impact. Plus, it is difficult to maintain a diverse group of employees if everyone hired is the same as the one doing the hiring or the one in the role already.

An objective approach is best, which helps to avoid some of these dangers. The temptation to meet with every employee referral will always be present, which is why it is so important to avoid giving in to this temptation. Employees are not offended or sad when their referral is not interviewed or hired, because they are just trying to be helpful by sharing jobs with their network. Most will recognize that there are specific requirements for the role. In fact, many employees, instead, tell me that they were shocked someone they referred was interviewed or hired, since they were not even sure it was the right fit to begin with!

There is no need to feel bad about *not* interviewing every employee referral. Expressing gratitude to the employee doing the referring and stressing the importance of employee referrals should always be at the forefront of any program. There are hundreds of studies that show how much of an impact gratitude can have on those that both give and receive this expression of appreciation.

STEP SIX: Recognition and Gratitude

Recognition for the help given by employees is the most important part of the program, which means there should be a level of consistency as it relates to the rewards being given.

Openly reminding employees of the reasons behind the program, actively recognizing and introducing the great people that were referred and hired, and expressing gratitude for those employees who referred and participated are key parts to ensure that the leader branch has all it needs to be the strength the tree requires.

Organizational leaders should be involved in this recognition whenever possible to validate the employee participation from a leadership perspective. Those leaders should either be the executive team or the manager of the department for which the new employee was hired. This approach helps reinforce *why* the program is paramount to the growth and strength of the entire organization.

Just like the roots of the tree system need to have a solid connection, the leader branch will be the foundational link between the trunk and all other branches of the tree for the rest of its life. Persistent acknowledgment becomes the propelling energy that makes the flywheel continue to move, pushing the circular motion into step one and consistently generating the most hires for any organization, thus demonstrating why it is considered the leader branch of the Hiring Tree.

The next branch is the second most important branch because it will often lead to a lot of applicants, it may just take some extra effort to sift through them. However, the quality of the applicants from this branch can be better by going back in time to understand some of the marketing principles that existed in the days of newspaper ads. The key is to nourish this branch effectively, which is why it is important to understand proper job optimization practices. This branch is one of the major reasons recruiting is, and always will be, marketing.

9

JOB OPTIMIZATION BRANCH:
Search Engines and Aggregators

W HEN FARMER PYNE snips away at his apple trees to remove the shoots and suckers, he looks for those core branches that have the right angle and the right girth to become the foundational branches that will grow and strengthen the tree, providing balance, as opposed to becoming a weakness to the tree.

Weak branches will break easily under the weight of the fruit they bear, creating an imbalance that could impact the fruitfulness of the tree during its lifetime. When this imbalance is not addressed from the beginning, the life of the tree is shortened, or worse, the fruit it bears is not a top-quality fruit that will attract customers for years to come. With this concept in mind, an organization will need to focus on some core branches once the leader branch is in place and effectively feeding the other branches.

The first branch stemming from the leader branch, as part of the organizational Hiring Tree, involves the use of online job boards, but more specifically, those that are considered search engines and aggregators. The most popular search engine is

Google,[10] and Google Jobs acts as an aggregator, gathering the links to millions of companies' positions across the country, allowing applicants to seek work through the platform. Indeed[11] is another popular job board, but it is important to understand that, at its core, Indeed is also a search engine, or what is known as a "vertical search engine" because it focuses on one area: job searching.

Many of the most popular boards today actually function based on search engine technology, which is important to understand in order to effectively feed this branch and help it produce the best fruit. This is another reason why a job description is ineffective when used on search engines.

A job description is typically not "search engine optimized," a popular term that is labeled as "SEO." There are three specific principles that need to be understood about how search engines work in order to use this branch in the most effective way possible. These elements are vital to writing job ads that are written purposely to be search engine friendly in order to maximize visibility and convert a job seeker into an applicant.

A search engine uses an algorithm[12] and artificial intelligence (AI)[13] technology that is designed to determine whether the job ad in question is the right ad to display when a search is conducted. When it comes to job search, this smart technology will display a list of jobs that matches what the applicant is seeking based on the keyword, pricing structure, location, radius from a zip code, and other factors that may be used as a part of the filtered search. In essence, the algorithm is designed to grade or rank the millions of positions based on the filter used by the individual job seeker to display those applicable roles which best fit the criteria selected.

The first thing to understand about these factors is that they are constantly changing. Much like the stock market, where prices go up and down based on a variety of factors, the algorithm is always evolving, trying to determine what the job seeker meant as they conduct their search. When a search does not go as planned, the job seeker may change the keyword used, modify the radius range, or adjust the salary range, etc., so that there is a constant shift in what gets displayed.

The algorithm is constantly working and adjusting and modifying the displayed results accordingly. When it is done right, the job seeker finds positions that truly match what they seek, and they tend to come back to conduct future searches based on the good experience they had previously. This is the ultimate goal of the search engine: to provide a great enough experience, so that the job seeker will come back to conduct a search later when the need to do so presents itself again.

The first principle to understand about the way search engine rankings work is that there is no magical secret sauce that will work *every* time, because the algorithm is designed to change and adapt to display the best results possible. What works today may not always work the same way six months from now. Many organizations that do not understand this basic concept struggle to understand why the job ad they used last year (which may have produced some great results) is no longer working.

The algorithm rules and ranking measures may also be impacted by scam artists. These individuals seek to post fake jobs to steal identities, to run affiliate scams, and to promote other malicious practices to make money off the disparity of job seekers trying to advance their careers or pay structures. Despite this practice, there are some core elements of a job ad that will benefit organizations the most, and these SEO concepts have not changed dramatically over the last two decades.

The second principle to understand is that the target audience of most search engines and aggregators is not the same as on traditional job boards. Traditional job boards, when they first started, focused heavily on employers for their revenue, which came about through the purchase of job postings, access to résumé databases to conduct searches, email campaigns to applicants, text campaigns, and other types of programs designed to attract job seekers to apply. Unlike traditional boards that focus on *employers*, the target audience of the search engine is the job *seeker*. This is why, when Indeed entered the scene many years ago, it very quickly became the board of choice to look for work, since job seekers flocked to the search capabilities to aid them in their desire to find work. Back then, Indeed did not require an account either, so many job seekers loved the fact that they would not get all the spam email or other forms of unsolicited advertising that caused many to get frustrated with the traditional boards of the day.

Over time, Indeed evolved, and now allows a job seeker to create a profile to aid in their submission process, so their main focus has been on the applicant experience, not the employer experience. If the job seekers do not have good experiences, they will not return to conduct future job searches, which means there is no traffic to prove value to the employer who wishes to have their jobs displayed in the search results. As you can imagine, this focus on the job seeker has helped to mold and shape the way job searches are conducted today, forcing traditional boards to evolve over time.

The third and final principle is to recognize that the employer can, in fact, have an impact on whether a job seeker chooses to apply. To better understand this principle, it is important to understand the job-seeking process that takes place on a search engine.

There are three steps a job seeker takes when applying for a job on a search engine: the impression, the click, and finally, the option to apply. The impression is the display of job ads in list form, based on the search parameters set by the job seeker. It is called an impression because the ad shows up in the list to virtually "impress" the job seeker, enticing them to click to learn more, thus introducing the second step.

This second step is where most search engines make their money from employers, hence the ad campaigns called "pay-per-click" campaigns. Clicks are very much like the stock market, because the value of a click will go up and down based on demand, popularity, and the desire for other employers to pay more for a click than another competing employer for the same keyword. The price paid for a click could be ten cents one day, forty cents the next, and then drop right back to fifteen cents on the third day. This is why search engines will typically have employers create a campaign "budget," where they are asked to allocate a set dollar amount per month, per week, or per day. As clicks occur, the current price of a click is deducted from the budget over time, until the funds are used up.

Indeed is also testing a new concept in 2022 in select areas called "pay-per-application," where the employer pays for each application received instead of the clicks on the job ad. The goal is to provide more value to the employer because they are paying for an actual applicant instead of the just the clicks on the ad. It will be interesting to watch this idea progress, and the good news is the optimization practices described in this book will continue to deliver quality applicant flow regardless of which campaign type the employer uses.

The final step is where the full job ad is displayed and the button to "apply" is highly visible, to encourage the applicant to make the decision to submit an application or send a résumé.

Most employers do not realize that they can influence two of these steps in a big way by playing the game of job optimization correctly. The job *ad* impacts *all* three of these steps, which again is why a job *description* is the worst way to influence results, improve visibility, move a job seeker to click, and then convince them to send a résumé (apply).

Job Optimization Practices – Search Engine Focus

The first search engine rule in writing a job ad revolves around the use of a good job title, which effectively becomes the main keyword the algorithm uses as part of the ranking process. This was discussed in detail back in Chapter 6 from the perspective of the applicant.

This principle of selecting an appropriate job title is critical to the search engine algorithm and problem-solving process, in order to aid the job seeker. As mentioned previously, careful consideration should be taken into account when selecting a job title. In my previous example about the sales role I was seeking to fill in two different states, the job title had a direct impact on the job seeker's ability to find my ad in the first place. The reason the job ad title is so important in SEO practice is because it leads us to the first principle of creating a search engine-friendly ad, which can directly impact the "impression" stage mentioned previously. I call it the "1 to 2 Percent Rule."

The 1 to 2 Percent Rule

In Chapter 6, the focal point was to please the job seeker by using a job title that would attract the job seeker and prompt them to click and read more. The difference here is that, now, our focus is on the algorithm. The goal is to help the algorithm understand what should be considered part of its ranking process of the ad itself. The job title becomes the first major keyword used throughout the body of the ad.

The reason this rule is called the "1 to 2 Percent Rule" is because this is the percentage of times the keyword should be used in the *body* of the ad. However, the goal here is to write an engaging ad and to not detract the applicant from applying, which is why it is important to understand this rule and the impact it can have on the search engine side of things.

To illustrate an example, I am going to use the experience

of one of my many credit union clients that will often place ads for tellers. The term "teller" is not that popular of a keyword, so part of the research here goes back to the roots we discussed at the beginning of the book. It is important to have a sound understanding of what the applicant will be *doing* in the role *most of the time*, since this can reveal some additional keywords that can be used in the job ad itself.

A teller is truly a customer service-oriented team member, since their main role is to effectively work with clients and provide the service they need. As banks and credit unions continued this research process, over time, the term teller changed to "customer service" representative or "member service" representative. This key word was much more popular than the word "teller," and this slight change has made a big difference in the banking industry to effectively attract applicants to these types of roles.

If "customer service" is my main keyword, then the term "customer service" should be used throughout the body of the ad, 1 to 2 percent of the time. In other words, if I wanted the algorithm to use the term "customer service" as part of its ranking process, and for my job ad to be readily displayed to applicants seeking a customer service role, then I need to make sure the term "customer service" is used up to 2 percent of the time in the job ad itself. If my ad is comprised of three hundred words, then the term "customer service" needs to be used at least three times, and up to six times, within the body of the ad.

The great part about this rule is that it can be used to target multiple keywords at the same time. In this same example, I may want to use the term "teller" 1 to 2 percent of the time as well, and possibly the word "support" or other relevant terms. As long as the "1 to 2 Percent Rule" is followed, multiple keywords can be targeted in the same job ad, even if they are not part of the job title itself.

However, I would caution any organization to avoid a concept called "spamdexing," or the more popular term "keyword stuffing."

Keyword stuffing is a term regularly used to describe the process of "stuffing" an ad with keywords so as to influence the search engine ranking and to cause the ad to appear first in the search results. This is why it is important *not* to exceed the 2 percent part of the rule. Too many keywords can also make the ad less effective at the "apply" stage of the process because the applicant can tell that the use of the keyword was a bit of an overkill.

Use of the keyword(s) should be a natural part of what is written. Many recruiters (including myself), when the concept of search engines first came out, they would take keywords and write them multiple times at the bottom of the ad in order to rank better. Competitor names were also added to job ads in this way to make their ads appear in searches by job seekers for a competitor! They would even go so far as to modify these keywords by changing the color of the wording to a white text (known as "white fonting"), so that they were hidden to the job seeker reading the ad, but not the algorithm itself.

Today these practices can not only demote the job ad (it *will* get caught!), but in many cases, can cause the ad itself to be fully blocked by the algorithm, which can be a painful experience to the employer when trying to remedy the situation.

It is important, when using this rule, that keyword stuffing is not introduced. If the initial principles, as outlined in Chapter 6, are followed (that of trying to attract the applicant to the job by following this important SEO rule), then the use of keywords in the ad should be fairly easy to do.

The final part of this section asks, "How does one research and come up with good keywords to use?" The first option has already been mentioned in the roots stage. Full conversations with managers and employees already in the role itself are, by far, the best way to determine whether there are certain keywords that are relevant and helpful to the job seeker.

The second option revolves around the use of online search tools.[14] Some tools have costs associated with them, so the employer can decide how they wish to approach this process.

The last option is to pretend to be a job seeker and begin conducting searches on a variety of boards to see what keywords are *suggested* when starting that search. While the suggestions themselves are not proven to be the highest-ranked keywords, they are, nevertheless, popular search terms by job seekers. This is the algorithm trying to be "smart" in its process to solve for the applicant's problem (finding a relevant job). It's kind of like when one is texting a friend or family member. The smart technology of the phone will suggest, or try to guess, what word is being sought, so that the one typing can easily select the word without having to type it out completely.

If the word being searched for (the job title) is not displaying as part of the "smart" list, chances are this is a keyword that is hardly ever used by job seekers, which may help to guide the employer in selecting a better keyword or job title that is more relevant. Keep in mind, too, that just because a keyword is not popular today does not mean that it won't be popular six months from now. This is why the research part of it is so important, to discover what is popular right now and relevant to what job seekers are looking for right now.

Again, the ultimate goal here is to select the right keyword(s) and then make sure they are laced throughout the job ad itself, 1 to 2 percent of the time. This is a great way to influence the algorithm to rank the job ad based on the keyword(s) used in the ad, which will lead to an increase at the impression stage of the search process. More impressions mean the job ad will display more often to job seekers, based on their search criteria. This can also increase the effectiveness of pay-per-click campaigns, when used by the employer, making the money spent much more effective in receiving better quality applicants. The same will apply to the new concept of pay-per-application campaigns.

The Refresh Fallacy

Craigslist is a popular website used today to post jobs and list other items for sale and trade. It is so popular that this particular board has created a false impression of how search engines work, due to its functionality. It amazes me, too, that sometimes the employees of many popular search engines sometimes give in to the idea that there exists the ability to "refresh" an ad, which magically pops the ad back to the top.

When boards like Craigslist first came out, this is exactly how they worked. In fact, as a recruiter, when I used this popular board and other similar boards, I would go and repost the job ads every three days. After reposting, my ads would appear at the top of the page again, giving them more visibility. I had a colleague that used to post or refresh a job ad every eight *hours* to take advantage of this concept.

However, if employers think that refreshing the ad every week or so is a way to boost their results on search engines, by causing their job ads to magically pop back up to the top of the page, they are sadly mistaken. It is disheartening when I hear a recruiter argue vehemently about this concept or try to convince others that this is how the search engines work, but this is not the case. In fact, if this is done excessively, there is a better chance that some of the major boards today will demote or block the ad altogether, due to a violation of terms of service, making this concept an important one to understand.

The algorithm is designed to use keywords and ad quality to determine placement, not the most recent date used in its creation. In fact, to test this, one can go to any search engine and conduct a search. They will notice that there is no order to the dates a position was posted, even though many boards will list how long the role has been available. Most engines, too, no longer display the time beyond the initial thirty days of the post, so it is hard to know truly how long it has been up on the job board.

I want to make the reader aware that, while this practice may still work on boards like Craigslist, this "refresh" concept does not exist when it comes to the intricate algorithms used when displaying search results to a job seeker. Most algorithms today will remove postings that are older than six months altogether, and after ninety days, many of these types of ads are not given as much visibility anymore. At the ninety-day stage, if an employer still needs to hire for a particular role, it is best to post a new ad. A job ad should never be taken down *and* reposted before the initial thirty days since some algorithms are designed to catch this, because this is a common practice of scam artists.

When an organization chooses to spend money on a job ad, the algorithm will automatically "boost" the ad to display more often on the first page or two of the search results in order to increase click rates and applicants applying for the role. When someone says, "Refresh my ad, please," they simply want to be displayed on the first one or two pages of the search results, which is why it can be attractive to pay the money required to sponsor or boost the ad. Money spent on optimized ads are much more effective than money spent on job descriptions.

Quality Control

Many search engines have quality control standards in place to ensure that the job ads displayed do not lead to a bad experience for the job seeker. These standards are heavily in place to avoid displaying ads listed by scam artists, who attempt to post fake job ads as mentioned previously.

Quality control is an ever-evolving process, due to the evolution of tactics scam artists use to try and "game" the ranking system. When search engine technology was first introduced, it became critical for recruiters to learn how they worked, in order to rank better and to be displayed on page one, which led to the keyword stuffing and other *bad* practices already mentioned.

The issue is that these types of practices led to an unfair ranking advantage and being displayed more often, which led to more applicants, due to the increase in visibility. The results were positive for the recruiter, but over time, the algorithms began to recognize these patterns and the smart technology evolved. Today, these practices can now lead to job ads being penalized or even banned altogether.

Knowing this, the most important element of quality control that most search engines adopt today is that of positively ranking *content*, using a unique algorithm to determine whether that content is unique, relevant, and helpful to the job seeker. This is why employers must also adopt a concept of transparency in their job ads to maintain this uniqueness and relevance to what the job seeker is trying to find.

Job titles are the most common places employers will try to "game" the system or add "clickbait", like how newspaper ads were used back in the day. The practice of adding clickbait terms in the job title like "bonus" or other "wow factor" words is common, but many search engines will only allow these types of words *if* the employer sponsors the ad. In other words, the employers with those types of words in their job titles must pay to use those words in the title. If a bonus *is* provided, it is better to include the bonus and information about the bonus in the *body* of the ad.

Realistically, though, this type of practice does not help with ranking, so spending more money to place these words in the job titles may not be the best use of an organization's resources. The simplest way to think about this is to answer the question "How often will a job seeker search using the words 'immediate opening' or 'shift one' and other similar terms?" The answer is they *never* will. When looking for work, the most common practice is to search using keywords that are relevant to the role they seek, which is why the job title is so important. Many applicants today also admit that clickbait words in titles will turn them off from wanting to click the ad.

Copycats

When I was a child, I used to bug my brothers and sister by mimicking them. They would shout at me and tell me to stop being a "copycat," but I would continue to egg them on until I'd achieved the desired result of annoyance.

Another quality control factor many search engines use today is a "copycat rule," which is as annoying to the algorithm as I was to my siblings. With today's technology, it is a very easy, and a well-known practice, to "copy and paste" information to save the time of typing out the same thing that has been typewritten before. However, when it comes to job ads, while this is a time-saving approach, it can hurt the ranking of the ad itself.

For example, copying a competitor's ad because the wording was well-written will not help the one doing the copying. The most common violation of this practice I see is the "about us" section of a job ad. The about us section of the job ad is typically copied and pasted from the company's website, or from other job ads that have been written in the past.

There are two challenges that present themselves with this practice. First, it is not *unique* content, which is something that the algorithms are looking for in order to determine quality. The second issue is that, when the marketing team wrote this section, they were writing it for a specific target audience, usually the consumer, *not* the job seeker. This produces an about us section that is not unique and which is targeting the wrong type of person to begin with.

If every ad starts the same way, with the same "about us" description, not only does this do a disservice to the job ad, it also does not help with search engine ranking. Whenever possible, the about us section should be unique to the company *and* the role. Part of the about us section should tell a story about the impact the role itself has on the organization. A story is much more powerful to the reader, because they can envision themselves in the role as it relates to how the role fulfills the needs of the organization.

This is exactly why I discussed in an earlier chapter the importance of working with managers to find out what their current employees love about their role and the company. In working with my own clients on this concept, many of them have found that different aspects of the organization stand out to different groups of people, which can also help with writing different versions for each role, to target multiple job seekers. This is the best way to make each job ad unique, and a great way to be inclusive and diverse in your attraction process.

Also mentioned in a previous chapter, not only is this creative, but it will also help your job ad ranking by being considered a *quality* job ad. I often tell attendees at conference sessions I teach that it really shouldn't be "about us" anyway. It should be about the job seeker. Maybe the section should be renamed "About You."

Ad Rotation and Radius Rules

I work with a lot of restaurant and retail chains across the country, many of which have been hit hard by the recent COVID-19 pandemic. Many corporate entities also have me work with their franchise owners, because franchise owners are not always great at hiring and are constantly reaching out to corporate for help.

The same goes for small business owners, who are so focused on their business, they have little time to figure out how to hire effectively. I see a similar issue with home health care and other "clinic"-type organizations with multiple locations.

There is a common rule that exists with some of the boards, known as the radius rule, and restaurant chains are well known for not only violating the copycat rule mentioned above, but also violating the radius rule, limiting their visibility. This rule applies mostly to organizations that have the same job listings for multiple locations *and* those locations are twenty-five miles or less apart from one another. When the same job ad, word for word, is used for the same position at another location and the other location is less than twenty-five miles away, search engines will truncate the ad.

This is why many owners will get plenty of applicants at one location and hardly any at the location just a few miles away. It confounds the franchise owner or the general manager, but what they do not realize is that they have violated both the copycat rule and the radius rule at the same time, creating a double whammy effect.

Instead, the franchise owner could just post one ad for both locations, even if the locations are separated by a huge bridge (like a client I have in New York), but while the locations are only a few miles away on the map, it could take thirty minutes to make the trip, not to mention paying for tolls. Not ideal.

Another reason this can be difficult is that you may have two different franchise owners in the same area competing for the same applicants, using the same job ad. One owner may get all the glory, while the other owner is left with little to show for their money and efforts, which is another reason why copycat practices can be harmful. The great news is, there is a way around this dilemma, known as "job ad rotation" (and for competing franchise owners, this includes not copying the other owner).

Job ad rotation does require a little bit of effort from the organization doing the hiring, but the rewards are tremendous. One of my favorite examples comes from a Batteries Plus[15] franchise owner, who was struggling to hire for two of their retail stores. After discussing the optimization practices already described herein, we created two different ads for the *same* position. At one location they posted ad version A, and then at the other location, they used ad version B. After thirty days, they rotated the ads, posting version A at the second location, and version B at the first location.

By rotating their ads in this way, they were able to increase their applicant flow for both locations by over 300 percent in three months. As you can imagine, the impact this had on their hiring process not only relieved a high level of stress for the owner, but it also made a big difference for her employees, who now had the extra support of coworkers to alleviate some of the responsibilities. This practice is also a great way to show the algorithm that because the ads are different, there is no need to block or truncate the ads from the search results, granting more visibility to *both* job ads and producing steady applicant flow.

Future Rules

Finally, it is important for the reader to understand that the rules of the game are evolving all the time. Scam artists, smart technology, artificial intelligence, and perhaps future technologies that are still unknown, will continue to help the hiring world evolve. As these rules change and evolve, it is important that organizations stay in tune to these new rules and learn to play by them well.

Many search engines that exist today have representatives that employers can work with to learn more about these changes. ApplicantPro is another good example of a tracking system company that not only provides software, but continually seeks to educate its clients on how to effectively market their roles to attract the applicants needed to grow their organization. Since this is the second strongest branch of an organizational Hiring Tree, following these rules will help this particular branch produce some exceptional fruit regardless of a drought or a bumper crop.

For the next branch, students will be the main focus. Sometimes this branch is not always the best fit for every position, but it is one of my favorite branches because I love the enthusiasm, fresh ideas, and passion students bring to an organization's Hiring Tree.

THE EDUCATION BRANCH:
High Schools, Colleges, Universities, and Specialty Schools

I LOVE VOLUNTEERING. This labor of love is a big reason why I have enjoyed working with SHRM for so many years, because my association with this society provides many opportunities to serve others and learn in ways that are not always available in the work environment.

In my experience as a volunteer, one of my favorite roles was as the director of college relations for the Utah SHRM[16] state council. This role propelled me into an environment of eager college students, filled with passion and hope for the future of work. As they prepared to live their own career paths, they were always seeking ways to network and connect with employers and experiment on jobs that became available.

There is no doubt high school and college graduates are the future workers for organizations across the country, which is why they are considered a strong branch of an organizational Hiring Tree. High school juniors and seniors are entering the workforce for the first time in their lives, eager to learn where their passions may lead them. Many specialty schools, tech schools, and industry-specific schools, designed to help students enter the workforce, also exist, different from some of the traditional school options.

There are program leaders, coaches, and mentors in these educational institutions who are highly motivated to help their students find work, which creates a unique opportunity for employers to network and become employers of choice among this group of potential job seekers.

The reason I brought up the idea of volunteerism at the beginning of this chapter is because networking with school staff may provide opportunities to volunteer time, talent, and expertise, which is a great way to develop a unique rapport with these individuals, which can help create a branch that works effectively. Some employers may not be able to hire these types of individuals in their organization, but the principles of good networking and volunteerism can still be beneficial in other aspects of the business, especially when it comes to hiring and finding quality people.

High School

Some students, depending on when they were born, will be as young as sophomores when they begin their working career. In some cases, like with my daughters, they may have started working in a family business at a very young age. As these students become young adults, many are excited to start dating and spending time with friends, exercising their independence and discovering who they are. They quickly realize that these aspirations are not a cheap endeavor.

This realization has propelled even those with less ambition than others to seek employment. I must admit, there is an element of satisfaction when a young man comes to my door to pick up my daughter for a date, especially when I know they are covering the events of the evening with money they earned on their own. I respect and admire those who work hard to earn a night out, even if it is on a meager budget. I love to listen to the escapades of the evening when my daughter gets home and shares the experience, especially when improvisation had to take place due to an unexpected budgetary restraint. Those have been the best stories so far!

Employers who are willing to employ high-school-aged young adults (in my experience) usually hire entry-level workers and seem to experience a high amount of turnover. As a result, it is a constant battle to fill positions and accommodate schedules for the busy times that come with the nature of the business. The restaurant and retail industry deal with this group of workers the most, but I am happy to say that, in the last several years, I have seen other industries expand into this youthful audience. They are young and inexperienced, but they are also eager to learn and grow and increase their capacity for contributing to society. It saddens me when I hear employers talk about this group as entitled, lazy, or flighty due to their youth.

Sometimes we forget that when we were that age, we were prone to similar mindsets, only thinking about the next few hours at a time. I remember many SHRM conferences, several years ago, that categorized workers into generational groups. While some of the presentations were a little comical in nature, new data has shown that it is more of an age group that defines us, not our "generation," even though there is some element of truth to generational gaps due to certain experiences.

However, it is hard to categorize everyone of any generation into one simple box with a list of bullet points describing how they are prone to act or manage their responsibilities in the workplace. The reality is that we are all diverse in many ways, and that diversity is not only due to the culture or country in which we grew up, but our parents' upbringing (or lack thereof), religion, experiences, attitudes, and a variety of other factors that impact the way we think and act in any given situation. The dichotomy of classifying people into generational groups does a disservice to everyone within that generation, especially when that mindset is so ingrained in the employer that it causes them to make false assumptions about certain job applicants. Accusations of "That's how they all are" may not fit exactly in the round hole that has been created for them.

High school youth entering the workforce seem to fit within this sharp division of sorts, but such assumptions often limit the employer from truly seeing potential applicants for who they are and what role they could possibly play in the organization. In other words, there needs to be more of a harmonistic approach when it comes to hiring today's youth.

Today's youth want exactly what yesterday's youth wanted: a chance to prove themselves and show their value, *even* if they do it differently than what is considered traditional. They will also seek ways to simplify, or potentially do it differently, because they are naturally more curious and experimental. I love to be surprised, especially when I realize my idea of how something should be done was suddenly accomplished, even though it was done in a different way than I imagined or expected.

In a previous chapter I shared the experience of how failure often leads to an understanding of how something should be done (or not done). Too often, rather than explaining why something should not be done a certain way, the employer observes the failure and feels justified that their way was right in an "I told you so"-type attitude. The focus is solely on the way it should be done, without equivocation, instead of focusing on being a loving and caring teacher, seeking to help the student see and understand for themselves and learn the "why" it is being done that way to begin with.

I have always felt this proverb is one to consider in situations like this: "If you give a man a fish, you feed him for a day. If you teach a man to fish, you feed him for a lifetime."[17]

This approach can make a big difference in working with the younger generation, instead of making certain assumptions about how a generation will always act and react to any given situation.

I recently had the opportunity to attend a JAG[18] conference in Dallas, Texas, where I participated in the first ever National Career Development Conference (May 2022). During this conference, I was asked to conduct an educational workshop on résumé writing and preparation, which allowed me to guide high school students on skills meant to empower them when interviewing with employers and applying for jobs.

The competitive events portion stood out to me the most. A variety of students had been asked ahead of time to prepare a presentation on a future career path they wanted to explore. Students were expected to research the career and then present their findings to a panel of judges.

Part of this presentation included describing the career, educating the panel on the schooling required for the role, explaining how they felt they would be a good fit for the career path chosen, and defining what they intended to do in order to be hired in the position they sought.

As a judge, it was an amazing experience to meet with several of these students and learn what really motivated them. More importantly, the responses to questions and ideas presented on how to proceed along the path they had chosen were innovative, thoughtful, and creative.

When given the right opportunity, high school students can be a powerful resource for employers. The key is to work with the students effectively through some of the mentors and other program leaders, which help to run similar types of programs throughout the country.

If an organization wishes to work with a high school, the key is to get involved with the school in a way that can help benefit the students, which then allows the employer to network and gain ambassadors (the teachers) for their organization, who can share open positions.

One of the aspects of JAG that I love is that employers seeking to work with students can do so by volunteering their time to judge potential competitions, provide mock interviews, offer résumé help, and other types of interactive activities or workshops. As a national organization, there are many states that have JAG chapters in select schools throughout each state. There are also other organizations similar to JAG that have programs which serve the same purpose, giving an employer a powerful option to find potential future workers by connecting with the teachers and specialists involved in these types of programs in a genuine way. Not only do these organizations have programs where business representatives can volunteer to help, but some businesses may find opportunities to provide new ideas or programs as part of this partnership, creating a unique opportunity for students in the program to gain additional experience with that particular employer.

Another conference I attended for JAG gave me an opportunity to meet the recruiting director for Tesla[19], who talked about his experience with JAG and the efforts they have made to give high-school-aged young adults the opportunity to learn new skills, become certified in some of their machinery required to produce their vehicles, and at the end of it all, to become the newest members of the Tesla team at their Las Vegas location.

Some high schools have career days, where students will propose business ideas and "sell" their services and items as part of a school fundraising activity for different clubs or other school programs. Employers can participate by donating items and becoming part of the additional programs offered during the events of the fair. There may also be sponsorship opportunities to help promote the employer services, granting brand recognition and visibility. Band, orchestra, choir, sporting events, theater, and other programs at the school may provide additional options that best fit the culture of the organization.

Finally, some high schools across the country are actively developing industry-specific apprenticeship programs to help students gain experience while completing school. Other high schools have partnerships with local colleges and universities, allowing the students to earn credits before they graduate from high school.

If these programs do not currently exist, an employer may want to consider creating one to allow students to gain valid real-world experience. This may require an explorational conversation with educators to create a program that can benefit students, too.

One of my clients, a manufacturing employer, worked with the local high school tool shop teacher to develop a program that allowed the high school students to develop real-world experience while completing their requirements to graduate high school. The organization even built a specific machine to place in the school to facilitate the training and certification for the students, providing a valuable relationship between the school and the company. The machine permitted them to develop a certification program to allow seniors, upon graduation from high school, to take the exam, which then granted them a position with the company to continue their career path if they chose to do so for at least one year (a guaranteed job!). On-the-job learning experiences like this become valuable to the high school involved, because it allows them to offer interested students so much more than just a diploma upon graduation.

Some high schools create competitions where students compete in creating business plans designed to be implemented in real life. In some cases, winners of these competitions may win scholarships to college, or even grants and funds to start the business they meticulously put together as part of the event.

The exposure to business professionals, CEOs, and other executives as part of this competitive process allows the students to develop networking opportunities early on, in whatever career path they choose.

An organization may want to start developing contacts and relationships with local high schools to determine whether there are ways they can get involved with this valuable source of potential job applicants.

College/University

Like high schools, colleges and universities are a great resource for not only entry-level candidates still attending school and upon graduation, but graduate programs may also provide access to a unique group of fully employed individuals going back to school to consider future opportunities. As in high schools, there are specific programs and majors tailored to certain positions within an organization, but in some cases, providing guidance and expertise in the organization's industry may also be a great way to help the school develop a class or program as part of the curriculum to enhance the students' experiences with real-world challenges.

The career centers in these higher educational institutions are motivated to prove that going to their school provides a certain percentage of their student's viable employment after graduation. This desire to prove value grants a unique opportunity for employers to develop relationships with schools and thus enhance their recruiting efforts. There are several ways to become involved.

The first way in which an employer can get involved with this unique group of students is to have their jobs listed on the school job board. In working with thousands of organizations across the country, I have noticed that there are two major student boards that stand out among many of my clients: Handshake and Symplicity.[20] As of the writing of this book,

Handshake claims over 1400 schools across the country use their board for students, and Symplicity maintains over 2000 participating schools.

Posting jobs to these two major boards is a great way to maximize exposure to students who may be seeking internships or employment after graduation. Many of the schools or institutions that do not use either of these two online job boards have a career center where employers can share jobs with the student body via email or other means. These boards do not really have an easy-apply functionality, but I am hopeful they will look to build such features to connect with tracking systems in the near future, especially because the newer generations entering the workforce rely on these quick-apply functions more than any previous generation.

This leads to the second way to get involved, which is connecting with the career center. Years ago, before I started my own career in recruiting, I met a man who came to speak to our classroom on debt consolidation and sound financial practices, which tied to my major in finance. He was representing his own employer and was granted the opportunity to speak to our class due to a relationship he had formed with our professor and the career center where I studied.

Patrick O'Hara,[21] who had been a headhunter on Wall Street, would eventually become my first mentor upon graduation. He educated me on the most effective ways to work with colleges and universities. While much has evolved since that time, relationships will *always* be the most effective way to work with educational institutions, something Patrick excelled at. This will also make the employer's name much more recognizable when jobs are listed and made available to the students.

There are three relationships that will lead to a successful partnership with those campuses where an employer may wish to employ future graduates.

The first relationship to focus on is the one with the school's career center. Sometimes these centers are focused on specific majors, such as the business school career center at my school, which was only a small part of the entire campus. Most career centers will have full-time staff and students that work for them, giving an employer a unique opportunity to connect with both types of people.

Many of these relationships lead to introductions to professors who interact with the students daily, which is the next relationship to focus on. It was this type of relationship that led to Patrick's developing a presentation for our class that was relevant to our major, leading to conversations with the students, the final relationship and ultimate goal.

These meaningful conversations with students will lead to the coveted new-graduate hire the employers seek. I was always taught that it is important to educate and provide value first. This helps to develop trust in any relationship, because there is no selfish motive evident when value is at the forefront of an employer's approach. The goal is to hire individuals based on the connections made, but similar to the Hiring Tree already discussed, the relationships provide the right nourishment to bear the fruit for this particular branch.

These relationships can lead to other valuable connections and resources too. Some schools have partnership programs that can help with diversity, equity, inclusion, and belonging (DEIB) efforts made by the employer. The career center can also help with scheduled outreach options (such as email or text) to promote open roles, internships, or other opportunities the employer may wish to advertise. Most of the time this outreach is free to the employer.

These opportunities can be enhanced when schools organize career fairs, giving employers an opportunity to sponsor a booth on campus during the fair. It was during these fairs that I often connected with the career center, which would help me organize several days of interviews with prospective students, who expressed an interest in our organization. Rooms were provided for free or a nominal fee, and I was able to conduct interviews right on campus. This made it easier for students since they did not have to travel far or make arrangements other than coming to school to participate. In today's atmosphere, there are also many virtual options available to help facilitate opportunities like this, but overall, students do highly value the face-to-face interactions.

The career center also allowed us to promote and conduct an information session on campus in the afternoon or evening, which was advertised to the students directly. We would bring pizza and drinks and provide a mixer-type environment for students to learn more about the organization, to socialize, and to ask questions of some of the recruiters or hiring managers that were able to attend the event. It was a great way to interact with members of our team in an informal setting, where students tend to ask more questions, and it granted my team members an opportunity to get to know them in a different way. Plus, it gave students an opportunity to learn about some potential career paths they may not have considered otherwise.

Many students I have worked with over the years are eager to learn about available career paths since, often, they aren't sure what they want to do just yet. What a great way to expose students to potential career paths that they may not have thought they were qualified for or that they did not even know existed. Job shadowing and mentorship programs allow additional opportunities for students to experience the work environment and culture of an organization.

Like the high school ideas mentioned previously, the career centers love to work with involved employers that are willing to help with mock interviews, résumé tips and education, classroom presentations, and other activities designed to give the students an opportunity to gain knowledge and experiences, which enhance what they are learning in the classroom.

Many campuses also have student-sponsored clubs and groups tailored to an organization's interests, because they align with the organization's mission or core values. This is also a great way to help develop programs to help students become certified or to gain valuable on-the-job experiences, which also allows employers the ability to influence and align these programs to current industry standards and requirements. There is no better way to support the local community than to provide experiences like this, which also feeds the employer with qualified applicants for workforce planning.

This leads to the final way an employer can work with higher educational institutions: the internship. Many years ago, when I met Ryan Kohler, CEO of ApplicantPro, he had been working on developing the code needed to build a system that now benefits thousands of organizations across the country. I remember walking into a room filled with code written on the walls. It was here that we brainstormed with a developer on features and concepts needed to make the system successful, to attract new clients, and to accommodate for the then-emerging mobile technology, which appeared to be the future of software.

It was the summer of 2009, and as I was working to develop a sales and customer service process for the organization to create revenue, we decided to hire an intern to assist me in my efforts. It became an internship for Priscilla, a student at a local university. Her husband was finishing school, and this became a great summer role that could help her family financially as her husband prepared to graduate and find full-time work. This gave her not only hands-on experience working with potential clients, but helped me, as one of the skills she possessed was the uncanny ability to take the thoughts in my head and write them out, to help outline and develop the process I was envisioning. Creating a written process that could then be replicated for future hires was a crucial part of our growth as an organization, especially in those early years.

An internship is a great way to allow students to have a real-world experience and to help guide them as they decide what they want to do upon graduation. Paid internships are much more valuable to students and are a great way to show commitment to their success. Priscilla's efforts have had a lasting impact on our organization, since those processes became the foundational principles of our sales and customer service departments still in use today. Priscilla had a skill set that complemented what we were trying to develop for succession planning, which made her short time with us an invaluable contribution.

Vocational or Trade Schools and Other Programs

This type of education is typically specialized for certain industries or vocations where specific certifications, practical skills, or expertise are required in order to work within that field. Depending on an organization's industry, they may find that these types of schools provide a much better type of applicant for their open positions.

There are also programs that the employer can develop, as mentioned previously, where the company itself creates its own specialized educational pathway to develop future applicants for their roles. Coordinating these efforts with trade schools and other forms of education is a great, and often less expensive, way to create a flywheel with the right type of momentum to develop future, qualified, licensed and certified workers. Just like the higher educational institutions already mentioned, the relationships built with these organizations are crucial to the success of any program developed or implemented.

The educational branch of an organizational Hiring Tree is such an important aspect of any business. I have yet to find an industry or an organization that cannot benefit in some way from tapping into the potential of this branch in their hiring efforts, even if the only part of this branch used is the internship opportunity.

Hearing fresh ideas from young, enthusiastic students is a great way to improve morale and can be a great support to the core values of an organization. There are also a lot of virtual programs now available throughout the country where certain niches have been developed to further enhance the use of this branch. I would encourage any organization to think of the concepts introduced here, as well as other effective ways to participate, whenever possible, with future students and young adults who will continue to enter the workforce with an optimism and an eagerness to grow and flourish in their own career paths. What a great branch to tap into!

The next chapter will focus on a branch that is often misused due to a misunderstanding of its purpose. This misunderstanding can lead to very few applicants, causing many employers to get frustrated and abandon its use altogether. Like other branches, for it to be an effective fruit-bearing branch, it needs to be used correctly, and dare I say, "socially acceptable?"

THE SOCIAL BRANCH:
Company Website and Social Media Channels

THE SOCIAL BRANCH of the Hiring Tree is one of the most misused branches. The misuse does not come due to any violations or abuse, but rather due to a misunderstanding of how to effectively use the various parts of this specific branch to effectively attract applicants.

For this branch to be effective, it is important to understand the purpose of each social media channel and the target audience of that unique website or application. Before going out on a limb with this branch, it is important to decide who in the organization will have access to the platform on behalf of the company. It is also important to have a backup, or multiple people with similar access, so that if someone should leave the organization, there is not a loss of access to the original account. Lost access can also cause the organization to miss out on the active followers, historical posts, and other costly efforts that have already been put into the platform.

I have seen rogue recruiters or marketers create an account for their employer without really taking into consideration the level of access necessary to run the platform and create real value for the employer. Having a good policy in place regarding this can also help protect the employer from any potential "misunderstandings" that stem from this process.

The Company Website

The first and most critical part of using this branch effectively starts with the company website. The company website will always be one of the most important parts of an employer's social game, prior to creating accounts with other platforms, since the website is where the employer can shine the most as it relates to attracting potential applicants.

The first thing to take into consideration revolves around the concept of search engine optimization, which is something that has been addressed multiple times already with other branches. One of the simplest options here is to include a button to click for jobs in *both* the header and the footer of the website. Employers are free to select the word they prefer, but it is important to know that the keyword "jobs" outranks most other keywords. Other terms, such as "careers" or "employment," can also be used, but again, the most searchable term is the word "jobs." To be even more specific, "jobs at company name" or "careers at company name" are also very effective, because they target both the word and the combination of words for searches done by applicants on Google Jobs, which is still the biggest aggregator in the world, and where a high percentage of applicants still begin their job search. This also allows the organization to rank high with the keywords for their company name and the term "job" tied to that company name.

When jobs are listed on the company website, they should not be a long list of positions that, when clicked, display a PDF file of the job ad, or worse, the job description! The challenge with this type of practice is that the PDF file is typically not going to help with searchability. The list of jobs is fine initially, but each individual position should have a single page dedicated to just that job ad.

The same optimization practices already mentioned previously apply here, but remember, ultimately, the "content" should be jobseeker focused. In most cases, the use of an applicant tracking system that understands the need for optimization will already house the list of positions and then a single page dedicated to each role, making this a very simple option. If an applicant tracking system is not used or does not have this option available, then a single page dedicated to each position is best, even if it does cause extra work for the website specialist who needs to make all the updates. This is another reason why an applicant tracking system can be beneficial, since this can be linked to the company website and will have all the optimization options already in place.

Some companies prefer to maintain an element of branding on the company page that houses all their open positions, so one of the temptations here is to use a framing option to basically "frame" the jobs from the applicant tracking system into a box on the company website in the careers section. While technology has made this a bit better over the years, framing is not the best approach here. Search engine algorithms will not pick up the information that is inside the frame, destroying any real options for the job ad content being seen by the search engine to begin with. I always cringe when an employer asks me to give them the jobs XML feed so they can add those jobs to a frame on their website, because this only hurts their ad visibility or availability to applicants in their job searches.

Finally, the website is the greatest place to house content as it relates to the organizational strategy for hiring. The goal is to establish trust and drive awareness of the organization and what it is like to be employed there. Company events can be highlighted, and pictures and videos can be posted. Community events and activities that spotlight the outreach of an employer can be shared and posted. Links to other social platforms, such as Instagram, Twitter, Facebook, LinkedIn, and others, can also be housed here to attract more followers so they can stay in the loop when new content becomes available.

Videos where employees and managers talk about what it is like to work with the organization are another great way to share company culture (something that was discussed heavily in the roots phase). Videos should last sixty seconds or less, since many sites can limit the length of a video post.

More detailed information about benefits can also be shared, along with stories and experiences about *how* employees live the core values of the organization. Sometimes, in human resources, we are so focused on documenting the day-to-day, that we forget to also document the exciting things that make people want to *come* to work every day. These are the most important moments to document, because they become part of the history of the organization, creating lasting memories that will have an impact on attracting future applicants.

I have seen many great people come and go from my current company, ApplicantPro. They all have great stories to tell, memories that they will take with them, and experiences they will continue to have. ApplicantPro recently made the 2022 Inc 5000 list for the tenth year in a row,[22] a feat that is not easily done, especially since less than 5 percent of companies who make the list maintain the type of growth rates high enough to qualify for inclusion five or more years in a row. What I love about this accomplishment is, at a recent company meeting, employees were invited to share their stories using the hashtag #myapplicantprostory, which can be searched today for those that would like to read some of the stories that publicly exist.

There are so many ways to celebrate, and the company website is a great start to this celebration.

Social Media Platforms – It's a Trap!

I know this may come as a shock to the reader, so I am just going to say it:

Companies should *never* post their jobs to social media sites.

There, I said it.

Now, let it sink in for a brief moment before reading my explanation.

I remember receiving the first invitation to join a new networking platform in 2005 called TheFacebook. Back then, it was considered exclusive, since college students could only join if they had received an invitation to do so by a current member. The invitees also had to prove that they had an email address for the university where the invitation originated.

My invitation came because I had been working with college students for my employer at the time due to my role as a recruiter to potentially hire new graduates. This was great for me, because I had just graduated in December 2004 myself, which meant I still had a valid school email address that I could use to get on board.

Compared to the other option at the time called MySpace, TheFacebook sounded much more valuable, because you could control the group of peers you connected with (college grads), and the data and social options made it much more attractive to find viable candidates.

I was responsible for developing a process to target college graduates to consider working in our organization's open roles. Every week, our recruiting team would meet with the marketing team to develop effective advertising ideas, attracting the right types of students to our booth at the fair or allowing them to connect with us, granting them an invitation to join our social network. It was an incentive to join an elite group, with the hopes of developing some solid relationships with potential job seekers that would lead to future hires. This became a foundational principle throughout my recruiting career.

Whenever a new concept is introduced into the job marketplace, especially related to employment, there is a disruption that occurs. Lawsuits will always ensue, and suddenly what sounded like a good idea becomes a taboo topic until the kinks are worked out. I remember attending several SHRM events, as well as other conferences, where social media was touted as the future of all hiring and that job boards would be done away with altogether. Just as quickly as it emerged, though, the social game was put in check, as lawsuits started popping up about discrimination, bias, and disparate impacts that began to creep into hiring processes in some high-profile organizations. This caused the use of social media to become a taboo topic among many human resource professionals, where many decided to wait it out instead of proactively finding ways to use this branch to increase the potential for hiring without causing a legal uproar. One of the biggest reasons for the initial failure using this medium as a source was due to the job market seeking to use it as if it was simply another job board. Social media platforms are *not* job boards.

Another mistake that I still see practiced by many employers today is that they are so focused on attracting followers for the company social page, that they forget that these followers are *not* the right target audience for employment. Some marketing team members refuse to post their company's jobs to their social media channels for the company for this very reason, and they are absolutely correct. Company followers are there to follow a product or service, not to be notified of open jobs.

Additional mistakes were made when "groups" were introduced on social platforms. Recruiters and other hiring managers would create job groups, and then an extreme amount of excitement would follow as the number of people joining their group skyrocketed. From there, they would post jobs and share as much as they could about their organization, only to find out that the only people joining their groups were other recruiters looking to post their own jobs for the same purpose. Again, not the right target audience and certainly not the correct purpose.

What I learned with TheFacebook was that a group could be used to share ideas, to help answer questions, and to share experiences with others. These groups were very effective at helping to establish trust, because the goal was not to be a job pusher, but to be there to answer questions and to help the candidate along the journey. Since I worked with a lot of students, many were not even ready to graduate yet, so this journey could take up to two years. Students stayed connected because being a part of the group provided value. It provided mentorship and networking. Even when I had members who were not interested in working for my organization at the time, they would still refer others to the group because of what they gained from being associated with us.

As mentioned earlier, the greatest use of social media is to use it the way any social platform is intended to be used: as a platform designed for the sharing of experiences, ideas, pictures, events, and thoughts with others.

Social media is most powerful when someone other than the hiring manager is the one sharing the good news. Likes are not enough anymore. The algorithms have evolved to give much greater weight to comments, other shares, and those interactions which attract new participants, thus displaying the post more often in the feeds. I sometimes think of it like a fight breaking out at the local high school. When the fight first begins, a crowd develops and those who are involved at the onset are the main witnesses to the event. Once things break up and calm down, the other students not present in the moment of the match, only hear the news from first- or second-hand witness accounts. Eventually, the fight itself is no longer a part of future conversations, much like the ripples of water that slowly disappear as the wave spreads across the lake. Every once in a while, it might be brought up as a "remember when" story, but the effects of the original account are never as grand as they once were. It will take a new fight to create a different level of excitement later for the next round of newsworthy shares and posts.

To powerfully use social media in a positive way, posts should include company events, successes, parties, celebrations, etc. Much like with the nourishment of an apple tree, it takes time to produce sought-after results. When there is good news to spread from within the organization, take time to celebrate and allow the posts to be shareable!

Where appropriate, tag employees or others involved in the excitement, and thank them publicly if they allow themselves to be tagged. Adding appropriate keywords to the post using the hashtag (#) symbol is also a great way to allow the algorithm to place the post in other searches conducted with the use of that hashtag. The celebratory posts can expose individuals within the network connections of the employees to the great things that are happening with the employer. The company should not be the one sharing job posts. *Ever*. When a job post is shared by an employee, there is a higher likelihood those within that network will be curious and apply because of what they have heard and seen about the organization already. The trust has already been established, and awareness exists due to the previous news already shared. Momentum has been built up to that point, leading to passive applicants who will apply when the opportunity is just right. This is why employee referral programs are much more powerful, with social media being used correctly to share the good news in a natural way, as already mentioned in a previous chapter.

To be most effective, responding to comments and other conversations on the posts is a great way to show responsiveness and make things feel more personal for potential followers on company social media pages. It is also important to understand that social media requires a certain amount of patience, because of the passive nature of applicants on these platforms.

Social media has expanded to be much more than just Facebook, which is considered by many of the younger generation to be an old and outdated platform, to be used strictly by their parents. At the time of writing this book, Facebook has a jobs area, where employers can post jobs for potential job seekers on Facebook. Hopefully, in the near future, more will become available about this option! Currently, it is a manual process for employers to post a job to their Facebook Jobs area, and it only functions via a redirect to an applicant tracking system or company website for applicants to then apply.

While this sounds a little outdated, the hope is that this will continue to develop over the next year or so. Companies need to make sure their Facebook company page is updated, but it is important to remember that the jobs section and company pages are separate on the platform for a reason.

Even Instagram can be an effective tool to educate followers on what it might be like to work for the organization, to get information out there, but it is not possible to create clickable links for immediate action from the job seeker, which is why it is not quite as popular for this purpose. However, this does not stop employees from sharing the good news with their network about their jobs and the great things they are experiencing!

Twitter is another medium for potentially attracting applicants but requires someone very actively posting and responding to engage potential applicants. The most effective employers using this medium have their own Twitter handle (account) that is just for career options and what it is like to work for the organization, including posts specifically related to the company culture and what a job seeker may experience and find by working for that employer. This can include information about the job application process, the interview process, videos and highlights of specific departments, company events, or community activities where employees might be involved. The idea of working for the company becomes an exciting option for many passive applicants who are watching and reading tweets, observing what is happening within the organization, and then when the timing is right, a move is more likely to be made by the applicant to apply. Being responsive and consistent with responding to comments and questions is a great way to engage and show interest in those who may become an applicant at some future date, just like with other social channels.

LinkedIn is another great place for hiring mid-level and higher educated professionals, and with their recruiter platform, it makes it easy to even search for potential applicants willing to discuss new opportunities, since users can mark themselves as "open." But this still means this audience is, for the most part, passive. Much like on Facebook, the jobs search aspect is purposely separate from the company page itself.

The first requirement for the use of LinkedIn is to make sure that a company page is created. This option is free to all employers, and it is recommended that the employer either connect jobs from their applicant tracking system to their jobs section on their employer page or add their limit of one job on the free version. LinkedIn also has a paid option, called Career Pages, which allows for much more in-depth options for showcasing the organizational culture, mission, core values, and other elements to help the company stand out as an employer of choice.

Potential applicants can also use their LinkedIn profile to apply easily without a lot of manual data entry, by adding the feature to the applicant tracking system itself. There are some applicant tracking systems that already have some great connections in place with LinkedIn, with more to come, based on new features being introduced to enhance the use of this particular social platform.

Finally, keep in mind that, much like Indeed, LinkedIn is much more productive when job ads are written in a way as to be search engine optimized, which includes quality content to answer the questions applicants will have about what it is like to work for the organization, as well as what is offered in selecting the organization as the employer of choice.

TikTok Résumés[23] was a pilot program that ran for a short time in the summer of 2021. Select employers participated in the social experiment to determine the viability of using such a platform to boost applicant flow and target entry-level and new job seekers that are just now entering the job market for the first time.

While the results have not produced any real usable data yet, the concept they were trying to introduce is not a new one. The use of video introductions, and other video platforms, to help facilitate the communication between employers and applicants has existed for many years. There is no question there will continue to be a strong place for video usage in allowing applicants to present themselves for the first time to a potential employer. In a way, it has replaced the concept of a cover letter, where the video itself becomes a cover *video* with which to introduce themselves. In a similar fashion, employers who take the time to create real, raw videos from employees on what it is like to work for the organization can go a long way toward attracting people to want to learn more.

I am excited to see how potential social platforms continue to evolve in such a way as to allow the younger generations entering the job market to contribute in a unique way, without the worries of bias and discrimination. There is no question that future platforms may also emerge and present themselves as viable options to help in recruiting efforts, but it will be important to pay attention to what platforms may serve the employer best in their efforts to target those job seekers that best fit their specific organizational needs. Seek to understand the audience, and more importantly, the specific applicant sought. This can be done using the concepts introduced earlier as the roots part of an organization's Hiring Tree.

Talent Networks

The concept of talent networks has been around for quite some time, and for the most part, may not work unless they function the way I had developed my Facebook group back in 2005 (which, technically at the time, was not considered a group, but more of my own network of connections).

It is a common trend I have seen since the days of Taleo back in 2006, where the goal was to capture the email addresses of potential applicants to market to them in an effective way as part of a recruitment strategy. The concept works well for very large employers, because those in the talent network purposefully join to stay in touch to hear about potential opportunities. The majority of small and medium organizations struggle to understand the purpose of such a network, and misuse it significantly, which is why they often will not see the results they expect.

The secret to an effective talent network is to *never* share jobs within the network. Email is a valuable nurturing tool, which was why the concept was developed, but applicants do not want to be bombarded with job listing after job listing.

When Indeed first entered the scene, unlike Monster and CareerBuilder, applicants did not have to create an account, which also meant they did not become part of some extensive list that would basically spam them with jobs all day, every day. In marketing, it is known as "ad fatigue," because the audience will begin to tune the messaging out. Candidates were seeing the job ads repeatedly, to the point that they almost got sick of looking for work and unsubscribed or got frustrated with using the old traditional boards.

For most employers, talent networks should be designed to give the subscribers an inside look into the organization, almost as if it were an exclusive club, much like the way The-Facebook started. The network should be used to build trust, brand awareness, and showcase the impact the organization is having on the local community, industry, or on the lives of the employees who work for them. The sole purpose is to allow the subscriber to decide, over time, if this is the organization for which they will want to become a member. What is shared within the network should elicit feelings and emotions that move or compel the potential job seeker to act by seeking to connect about employment. This is the only way to effectively develop a talent network that will have the ROI an employer seeks.

In fact, an employer should be selective about the applicants within their talent network and only allow certain people to subscribe. These would be those applicants who seem like a phenomenal fit, or possess an incredibly needed skill set, but the timing just isn't right. The goal is to stay in touch and nurture the relationship until the "opportunity meets the effort," which is my favorite definition of luck. Instead of sending a rejection email to invite the applicant to check back later, there may be select candidates where it would be appropriate to invite them to become part of the talent network.

When I was a recruiter, I used to have an Excel spreadsheet filled with thousands of contacts that I felt were great applicants for their respective skill sets. Each sheet represented an industry, a skill set, etc. I even built macros into the sheet so that I could automatically message my homegrown "talent network" to stay in touch. My calendar was filled with alerts to trigger these messages to go out when I needed them to be automatically sent out. The goal was to stay in touch occasionally, so that a relationship was built over time.

When someone in my talent network was suddenly available, I would be one of the first people they thought about, because I had stayed in contact. Not because I always had the right position ready for them, but because the relationship had been established *and* maintained without force and without gimmicks or nagging.

I had an incredible talent network of acquaintances, and I was never shy to introduce someone to another within the network if I felt they'd be a fit for a potential mentorship or that they could receive help from one another. When someone was introduced to another, a conversation was more likely to take place, to at least determine compatibility. At the end of the day, I wanted to help. I wanted to be a resource and to potentially make a difference in someone's career journey. Changing jobs can be a major decision for the applicant, including their spouse, or their children, or anyone else that might be a part of their life. That is not something that should be taken lightly, so recognizing that it may take time is so important. Connections are what a talent network is all about. People helping people through connecting, since relationships are still the most important aspect of any group of people.

One of the last ideas that made my talent network effective was that I had segmented the list. What this means is that it is best to break the subscribers into "segments" as described in the marketing world. I did not know what segmentation was back then, but this was the very principle I was following in developing this list.

By breaking the list into segments, the messaging that went out to these different groups was tailored to what would be appealing to a particular group. Of course, there were some general messages that applied to *all* groups, but often, the segmentation was much more effective because it provided very specific and intentional content. This will be much more appealing to the audience when it is designed to be specific to their tastes.

This also means that time should be taken to understand those individuals that are part of the talent network. For me, it was an actual phone call or interview which led to a lot of the revealed information needed to segment properly, making it a much more personal experience. However, even a brief survey, which could be filled out when they subscribe or become a part of the network, may be sufficient to gather some basic information up front to segment the list in a meaningful way. One of my favorite things to do today is to include video as a part of shared content, something that was not readily available to me back then. Short and to the point is best, and I love how video can also help it feel much more personable.

An organization can develop this type of talent network, which truly supports this part of the branch to be a successful one. The key is to understand that it is a long-term solution, not a quick, short-term solution. Social media is similar. These types of networks require the patience needed to wait upon the fruit, much like an apple tree, which can take up to five years before it bears the delicacy that awaits the farmer! But once the tree is bearing fruit, it is a lot easier to maintain the tree and keep it producing fruit year after year, due to consistent effort.

The last branch is like HR because it is a graft, but not at the base of the tree. It is a grafted branch because it is not part of the original tree. This specific graft is placed in areas of the trunk or is placed at the base of strong branches. There are aspects of this branch that can produce some fruit and should not be ignored, which is why it is the final branch discussed in this book.

THE GRAFTED BRANCH:
Customers, Vendors, Competitors, and Search Firms

THE CUSTOMERS OF AN ORGANIZATION, the vendors they work with, the search firms they use, and even the competitors they may spar with, all make up what is known as the grafted branch of an organization's Hiring Tree. As an apple tree begins to grow, there are times when the tree may require another type of graft, specifically with the branches, to help when other branches are not quite producing the fruit desired. Often, a graft can strengthen the tree, allowing the other branches to blossom, because it helps the tree to become more resistant to disease and insects, creating a hardier tree.

Farmer Pyne also uses this concept to help shape the tree to its desired size and girth to allow for maximum fruit production. The shoot grafted into the stock of the branch is called a scion (pronounced sī-en). The root of the word comes from the concept of a descendant who is of a wealthy or influential family and is sometimes used to describe an heir. In the case of apple trees, it is a way to graft a strong, healthy branch into the tree.

Choosing the correct scion branch to graft into the tree is done during the winter months while the tree is dormant. The selection process for the scion is important, because the branch must be straight and smooth, about the width of a pencil, twelve to eighteen inches in length, and it should also have a few dormant buds on it to ensure that it will have the ability to blossom when springtime arrives. The interesting thing about this process is that the branch cannot be grafted into the tree until the spring, which means the storage of the scion is just as important as the selection process. Kind of like the heir waiting for the wealthy inheritance! The scion should be stored in the fridge to stay cool and moist and should be wrapped in plastic with sphagnum moss and moist paper towels. Eventually, this branch will pass on its qualities to the whole of the tree, which is why the quality matters.

In the business world, companies will develop relationships outside of the organization. Customers, vendors, competitors, and staffing or recruiting firms will make up most of these relationships and can provide a tremendous amount of value. Much like the graft of a scion into the apple tree, these associations can give strength to an organization's Hiring Tree as the company continues to grow and increase its influence in the marketplace. Below are some things to consider when it comes to these "scions" in business.

Customers

Customers are some of the best-quality scions that exist for the organization because they are already users of a product or service and can be great advocates for the company. They know what it is like to work with employees of the company, because they deal with them often enough to know what the experience is like. These relationships can lead to a natural way of sharing job openings with their own network of friends and family because of the great experience they have had.

Social media can play an important role here, too, where sharing experiences, events, and other employee experiences could then lead customers to sharing their own experiences. Customers are often some of the best followers of the company platforms. This is most definitely a passive applicant source, and customer reviews do have an impact on the research made by potential applicants, making the customer experience an important part of attracting top talent.

I have seen some organizations even offer rewards, similar to employee referral bonuses, for sharing roles within their network. This is certainly not necessary, as it is important that it not appear like desperation on the part of the employer, but may potentially add value to the idea of saying *thank you* for the referral. Most organizations that have these programs do not even market the fact that they *provide* a bonus, but they do pay it out and make it a public statement by making a big deal when the reward is given.

Like with employee referral programs, when service, support, and products are done well for the consumer, they naturally want to share their experience with friends, which can inadvertently lead to interested job seekers. Even if they do not actively share, potential job seekers may ask consumers about experiences, which can help those applicants that might be on the fence.

Vendors

Vendors are another potential source of referrals because they are similar to customers, since they also interact with employees of the organization. When an opening becomes available, they, too, are likely to share positions within their own network due to the outstanding relationship they already have with the organization. Like customers, these applicants tend to be more passive, so good experiences with the vendors can go a long way.

With SHRM, I have had the opportunity to attend a variety of conferences. Often, I am attending a show as a vendor myself, and I love to interact with the other vendors to learn about what it is they do. It is important to note that, as with a job fair, an organization should send their best ambassadors of the organization they have to represent the company at conferences. Having gone to these shows myself, I love the vendors I have met over the years, some of which have become very good friends, even if their product didn't fit within the realm of what I needed. Developing relationships can make it so that, when a need *does* arise that fits, people are already connected and can introduce individuals to one another.

Sometimes this connection will even lead to the vendor employee seeking employment with the company because of the great experience they have had. This recently happened with a friend of mine, who had experience with another vendor. When a role opened, it was a great fit for her to make the move into a similar space.

LinkedIn is my favorite place to keep in touch with vendors on a professional level, as it is an easy place to share open roles in a natural way, in case someone within their network is open or actively looking.

Competitors

Approaching applicants employed by competitors can be kind of tricky because of what I call the "poach approach." Poaching in the hunting world is an illegal activity, so the word itself already conjures up a negative connotation. In many ways, it can leave a negative taste in the mouth, similar to biting into an apple that is not ripe enough. An unripe apple has a starchy taste to it, ruining the experience of a crisp, sweet, and juicy expectation. Farmer Pyne would equate it to birds that relentlessly peck away at really good apples, making the apple no longer a viable piece of valuable fruit to take to the market.

Realistically as a recruiter, I have never been opposed to poaching an employee from a competitor if the offer is a better career move for the candidate. This can help the individual along their own career journey, but I believe strongly that there is a tactful approach. It shouldn't feel like pecking birds or an illegal hunt. It also opens a vacancy for another applicant to fill the role with the competition.

There are also times where the competing business is struggling. Once, I was able to recruit a handful of employees from my previous organization. It wasn't because I was actively going after them, but because my relationship with them was strong enough that, when they were open to making a move, it was like the low-hanging fruit of an apple tree, granting me the grace of a juicy, crisp experience. They reached out to me for help. Sometimes non-competes or non-solicits can prohibit this activity, so it is important to be aware when the applicant being interviewed is under such obligations.

On the other hand, more positively, sometimes the competition is not doing well, and may be relieved to know another competitor could help their former employees during an unexpected transition. Layoffs or other company circumstances could suddenly open a window of opportunity for one organization to hire some of the competitors' employees who are making an exit.

Sometimes it is not a direct competitor, but the unstable atmosphere of another local company, as mentioned in a previous chapter, that causes their current employees to feel they no longer fit that company's culture or environment. I have worked with many organizations over the years where someone hated the role they were in, and then, several months later, I worked with another person in the same role with the same company, only to find out that they were thriving and loved their new job. This is important to understand, because not everyone is a good fit for every organization all the time.

People can change. Circumstances can change. Relationships can change. Competitors can change. The company itself can change. Not everyone will like or connect with every opportunity available, and that's okay. In fact, over the years, I have had many coworkers leave and go to competitors, and I couldn't be happier for them. Whenever the opportunity presents itself, I reach out to see how things are going, genuinely excited about where their new role has taken them. They also continue to advocate for our company, and even refer applicants for open roles because of the great experience they had while working for us, and the mutual respect as they were exiting.

When bitter feelings and resentment cake the recruiting or off-boarding process, that is when it is time to consider whether the anger and frustration should linger, or whether it is simply time to let that apple fall to the ground and then look upward to focus on the next apple that is just about ready to be picked.

Search Firms and Staffing Agencies

There are times when an organization has exhausted all resources to find an ideal applicant for a role, but no fruit has ripened enough to fill the position. This is often true for staffing agencies that can help fill some quick positions that need immediate attention. Some agencies can also help with an applicant that has a specialized skill set, a specific educational background, or other unique qualities that are not the easiest to find. When there is a level of confidentiality to fill a role, a search firm can prove very effective. Other reasons may exist where using a third party can prove very effective.

When a position goes unfilled, others within the organization may need to make up for the work not getting done. This can add a tremendous amount of stress and pressure on employees. The supervisor will also have to step in to help cover duties and responsibilities, and the hiring manager will put forth a tremendous amount of effort to fill the role.

Frustrations can build up to a breaking point, sometimes ending in an outburst of anger, leading to a loss of another great employee or manager. Resentment may linger on for months and may be difficult to mend.

Much like with the scion process described earlier, care should be taken in selecting an appropriate staffing agency or recruiting firm to take on this task of filling a vacancy. The expense can be more than most smaller employers can afford, but overall, it may be worth it to keep things afloat. The key is to not act out of desperation, since this can cloud one's judgment. However, there are always two options: use an agency for a need from time to time or develop a longer-term relationship with an agency to help with ongoing needs (a practice I see often with manufacturing clients I work with).

I would highly recommend treating the process like selecting a scion, which means evaluating which type of firm or agency is required. The very first place I would start is to understand where the potential agency or firm generally acquires their applicants. If they are just posting and sponsoring ads to places like Indeed, an organization may be better off doing the same (unless there is no time or resources to do so). I have learned over the years that many agencies know how to use the principles mentioned in this book effectively, which makes it easier for them to attract applicants from the places the employer may already be posting. As a result, the price paid can be high.

Another important aspect is who the employee will work for. Are they going to be working for the agency or the firm, or will they be employed by the organization? Will it be a temporary placement, or will there be an option for permanent placement if the company desires it? For smaller employers, there may be benefits to having them employed by the agency, which could save on human resource expenses that may not currently be available. This should be clearly outlined in the agreement, so there are no questions later in the process. Since not all grafts take, like the scions, sometimes having the ability to remove a rotten hire when needed can be helpful.

One of the biggest challenges is finding a staffing firm or recruiting agency that can take the time to truly understand the organization, its culture and environment, and take on the task of helping to identify those job seekers that can fit within those parameters. Part of the vetting process should include the steps the firm or agency will take to understand the role *and* the organization. Much like the roots part of the Hiring Tree described previously, if the agency does not care to take the time to understand the same elements that were outlined in the roots section, I would be very cautious about signing a contract, because it could be more about making money from the situation than being a true partner in helping to fill the role for the organization.

Quality Fruit Requires Time, Money, and Patience

Farmer Pyne recently shared a post that I found to be contradictory in a way, but after carefully listening to his explanation, I found it an extraordinary practice to enhance the fruit he seeks to bear for his valued customers. The post featured an image of an apple tree decorated with hundreds of apples, in their infancy, growing on the tree. However, scattered on the ground, were almost as many apples. They appeared to have *fallen* to the ground, making the scene a potential nightmare. However, they had been *purposefully* removed from the tree by hand! In horror, one might ask, "Why was this done?" I love his comment on the matter since it is so relatable to recruiting in a deep and meaningful way.

"In order to have good-sized, quality apples, the tree cannot be overwhelmed trying to take care of too many at once. The apples just won't get the nutrients and attention they deserve. They would also take longer to ripen and may never reach a marketable size, color, or even the right taste for selling. In some cases, the tree limb itself may become so overpowered, that it breaks, ruining the branch of a very valuable tree. Quality fruit requires a lot of time, money, and patience."

I feel like these words of wisdom from Farmer Pyne truly sum up all the branches of an organizational Hiring Tree. In the world of hiring, too often companies think the best approach is to grow as many apples as possible. It is kind of like casting a wide net in fishing, to gather whatever happens to land in the net. This is exactly why posting a job *description* is such a bad practice. No time was spent in creating a job ad designed to target specific applicants, but rather, a blanketed description was thrown out there to just get some fruit on the tree.

Not all fruit will benefit the branch of any given tree, but instead, will potentially overwhelm the tree to the breaking point if not thinned. The money spent on workers to hand pick the right apples to remove from the tree is a valuable practice, magnifying the taste and quality of the fruit that remains.

What happens to all the removed apples that fall to the ground? They simply become additional nutrients and a natural compost, so the tree can continue to produce the best quality fruit fit for the organization for years to come.

From this point, the remaining fruit needs to be nourished until maturity. Patience is such an important practice as an organization develops their own Hiring Tree, which will continue to produce fruit, year after year, as sound practices and marketing principles are followed. When the focus is on the quality of the fruit and the experience of the fruit, the fruit will be as crisp, juicy, and delightful as desired, because it was planned that way from the beginning.

Just like Farmer Pyne focuses on quality control and the experience of the fruit, a similar focus should be made to enhance the candidate experience during the hiring process. In sales, we like to describe this as the customer journey. For the job seeker, this journey is called the hiring process, and it is sometimes overlooked or ignored. In fact, it is in this journey, where applicants will sometimes mysteriously disappear, never to be heard from again. The common term for this kind of experience is called "ghosting," something we will cover in our final chapter of the Hiring Tree.

13

A GHOST STORY

I HAVE ALWAYS BEEN FASCINATED by ghost stories. I remember the first time I really listened to the song, "It's the Most Wonderful Time of the Year," as sung by Andy Williams from a large, box-shaped record player in which my mother would "drop the needle" as school subsided and Christmas season began. With marshmallows toasting during a holiday party, and carolers singing in a snowfall I had never seen before (I grew up in Las Vegas, Nevada), I was intrigued to hear within the song that the evening would end with the telling of "scary ghost stories" with loved ones gathered to listen to the intriguing tales. It was a chilly evening in November when my family gathered with Farmer Pyne's family at the end of the apple season to share stories over a bonfire in the middle of his orchard, which led to the beginnings of the analogy for this book.

I begged Farmer Pyne to share with me any ghost stories from the orchards, but to my dismay, there were none he could recall. Despite this, we got to talking about the concept of "ghosting," which is where an applicant stops all contact with the organization, providing no explanation as to why. When related to applicants during the interview process, or even the ghosting done occasionally by employees, he admitted to me that this "ghosting" phenomenon has also troubled him in his own business.

This realization excited him a little, as he had, in fact, experienced ghosting in his orchard when I explained it in the context of hiring and employee retention. He brought up some very interesting facts about the apple trees that became relevant to the conversation. There are times when Farmer Pyne will go out to the orchard in anticipation of finding newly ripe apples ready for picking, only to find that some are suddenly missing. When I questioned him as to the reason why, he mentioned that this can sometimes happen because the apples are left on the tree too long, and the weight of the apple finally gives way in the wind, due to a weakened stem. Another reason can be attributed to the birds or animals that remove the apples by constant pecking or generally forcing them to fall, in order to haul them away. Sometimes the apple doesn't get the right amount of nutrients, so it doesn't have enough strength to stay on the tree, eventually falling off before it is ripe enough for harvest.

The scariest thing of all is when the tree is not thinned properly or taken care of. While it may produce a spectacular display of blossoms as spring begins, those blossoms never turn into fruit, and the tree remains barren for the entirety of that season, creating a lost opportunity for the tree altogether. Farmer Pyne, in relaying this last explanation, pointed out to me that sometimes the ghosting of an apple cannot always be blamed on the weather or other external circumstances, but is, perhaps, his own fault due to his own neglect.

To avoid future ghosting caused by this mistreatment, Farmer Pyne described to me specific adjustments he has made to the experience of the apple trees to make certain that the ghosting is limited and less frequent. As with Farmer Pyne, it is important, as an employer, to understand that not all ghosting can be avoided, but some ghosting can be controlled by making some simple adjustments to the candidate experience during the hiring process.

As the concluding chapter in this book, the reader will now learn how to become what I call a "Hiring Ghostbuster," which includes a sound understanding of concepts that can be applied to all branches of the organization's Hiring Tree, since all branches can be impacted by this mysterious and eerie phenomenon of a job seeker suddenly "disapparating."

Manager Engagement During Interviews

In a recent Gallup article,[24] the variance in employee engagement is about 70 percent, proving that the manager is the key influencer and the one who determines how effective that engagement can be. I have found in my own research that this is the same percentage as it relates to the hiring process, especially when the hiring manager is fully engaged in the interview itself. Since hiring managers are the ones responsible for relaying information about the organization, especially when this information is directly tied to the potential employee's job, this can have a tremendous impact on ghosting that occurs during the interview process.

Many hiring managers, human resource professionals, and even business owners are so buried in administrative tasks and processes, that, by the time the moment arrives for the applicant's interview, the experience is a deflating one. Applicants are very keen during the interview process and can tell if the hiring manager is engaged and present in their meeting (whether by phone, online, or in person). If a manager is distracted, unfocused, and interrupted during the interview (via phone, text, or physical encounter), it creates an element of angst for the applicant, who may already feel nervous as it is.

The hiring manager should be fully engaged in the process, giving every ounce of attention to the individual in the room, on the phone, or in the online meeting. I have often heard managers relate their belief that the applicant should be "grateful" to have received an interview, regardless of the experience. The problem with this attitude is that it almost sounds like they are saying there is a surplus of qualified applicants, and therefore, applicants should be willing to go through whatever the hiring manager feels is necessary.

Hiring managers are also the brand champions and ambassadors for the organization, as mentioned in a previous chapter. Their main role is to paint a picture for the applicant as to what it would be like to work for the organization. They should also be able to answer all questions, without having to check with someone else and get back to the applicant later. As leaders, they should know the answers, since they are the decision-makers within their own department or organization. Compromising this influence can cause an applicant to question whether this manager is knowledgeable enough to manage effectively. These doubts can easily lead to ghosting, because the applicant is unsure, especially when faced with another job offer or interview experience that was much better overall. Proper preparation for all potential questions is a great way to demonstrate this influence, eliminating potential doubts that may emerge.

One of my favorite examples of eliminating doubts comes from *A Christmas Carol*, by Charles Dickens (also one of my favorite ghost stories). Scrooge's experience as an apprentice under the direction of Mr. Fezziwig illustrates the importance this influence can have on job seekers and employees alike. There was no better picture painted than that of his boss, who took care of Scrooge, and at the time, Scrooge was happy to be a part of the business and contribute in any way needed.

One Christmas, when Mr. Fezziwig asked him to close the shop, Scrooge was eager to help set up the decorations for the coming party, where everyone was invited to participate, including other employees, clients, and neighbors alike. What a great example of a manager whose focus was on the individual, for at the end of the party, Mr. Fezziwig purposely thanked each guest as they departed. There is no doubt in my mind that those conversations were personalized, leaving each guest with a unique experience and a feeling of appreciation for all they had done to contribute to the success of this man.

As Scrooge recalled the event, watching it unfold, and even participating in the merriment, he suddenly remembered that he was there with the spirit. Looking towards the spirit, Scrooge heard him say, "a small matter to make these silly folks so full of gratitude." While a small matter to some, it is grand in the eyes of those experiencing such a moment of time with a great manager, especially in those first moments during an interview, where the applicant is forming a first impression of what it might be like to work for them.

The reasons given by Farmer Pyne at the beginning of this chapter illustrate some important points that have now been addressed. If an apple is left on the tree too long, it will eventually fall off the tree. The same thing happens to an applicant when the interview process is too long, or expectations are unreasonable. The candidate will just "ghost" the employer, since there are doubts due to a lengthy, drawn-out process.

When birds or animals agitate the apple on the tree, it may give way and fall to the ground. A candidate during the interview process may be experiencing similar outside influences that are trying to pull them away. Painting a picture and creating an engaging and positive experience is so important to keep these external influences from pulling the applicant away. Full transparency during the interview and outlining clear expectations of the role are important parts of the "big picture." Some organizations will introduce applicants to future coworkers, which is a great way to instill the confidence they might need to feel good about the role. This may help them overcome reservations about moving away from their current role or situation. The observations made by the candidates during these meetings can help them in the decision-making process, personalizing the experience.

When the apple does not receive the right nutrients, it may not grow to maturity and is lost early on. For the applicant, the "nutrients" are answers to questions and a feeling of confidence in the manager(s) conducting the interview. Some of these nutrients are provided in the job ad prior to the interview, which is why the job ad itself mitigates ghosting prior to meeting with the applicant, leading to fewer "no shows."

Frequent Communication

Another "nutrient" is that of communication during the hiring process. Additional questions may come to the mind of the applicant, requiring additional attention. In my research on this matter, most applicants prefer constant communication, which, on average, was defined as every other day. This step is important, even if the communication is to simply let them know there might be a delay, that other interviews are being conducted, or that other steps are still pending. Even when letting applicants know their journey in the process has concluded, applicants crave to know where they might have stood in the process.

Communication is also accomplished through a concept called "internal accountability," since some communication must happen internally during the hiring process. In essence, a hiring manager, or those involved in the interview process, should be accountable to a pre-defined set of rules. Developing a timeline prior to the interviews with potential applicants, can help managers stay engaged, thus holding them accountable to what they agreed upon, prior to starting the process.

I have often heard from HR that managers cause unnecessary delays during the interview process. While not all situations can be avoided, holding hiring managers accountable is much easier when the timeline and rules are agreed upon up front. Internal accountability can help stop ghosting from occurring due to fewer delays during the process, creating a much better experience for the applicant.

The Blame Game

I have questioned thousands of managers across the country on who is to blame for ghosting, and more than 80 percent assume that ghosting is the fault of the applicant alone. In response to my inquiries as to why this occurs, I have heard remarks about the way certain age groups act, or other false assumptions, that are not founded upon facts. These assumptions and generalizations can lead to ghosting, because individuals within those groups are being treated as if they have already committed the act. These managers fail to recognize that the blame can also be found in the process itself, including the attitudes of those conducting the interviews. The action of one applicant does not define an entire population, ethnic group, age group, or any specific applicant pool.

By the same token, what a manager *wants* and what is truly required for the role, does not always align. This is the reason the roots section described in this book is so important prior to seeking out potential applicants. Recognizing the difference between hard qualifications and preferences is the best way to alleviate these menacing inferences from creeping into the interview process, which can lead to a high probability of ghosting.

Farmer Pyne was keen to point out that organizations ghost applicants all the time, shifting a percentage of blame to the employer. In my own research and discussions with job seekers, over 90 percent of applicants define being "ghosted" by the employer as not even getting a rejection notice after they have applied. This means employers have been guilty of ghosting applicants for years. Rejection is part of the communication process and should be done swiftly once a decision has been made, so as not to string someone along. Applicants also observe not being addressed expeditiously as being ghosted.

Helpful feedback can be most beneficial to the experience of a rejected applicant, even when the feedback is truncated by legal requirements or the employer's fear of being more specific. If rejection is part of the experience, then careful consideration should be made when sending out rejection letters, especially to those who have progressed to certain stages of the interview process.

Individualizing the process for every applicant is important to all job seekers. They are not just numbers. They have families, aspirations, dreams, and, ultimately, they are seeking a work-life balance that will propel them to find success in their future endeavors in all areas of their life, including work.

Future job seekers have begun to enter the workforce, and the individualized experience is more important to this new generation than ever before. I love this comment from a Gallup article[25] that sums it up nicely as the future of work is considered: "Individualized information is important to everyone. But it's really important to millennials. More so than any other generation, millennials need to be in the loop about their day-to-day work, their part in the organization, how they contribute to the purpose, and where the company is headed." This aligns well with the information gathered during the roots part of the process of an organizational Hiring Tree. This will solidify the information that the newer generation entering the workforce will need to hear consistently in order to find success and feel that they are contributing to the organization in a meaningful way.

There is no need to give in to notions that may be limiting an organization's ability to allow a personalized experience, leading to an increase in ghosting. By mitigating the ghosting issue, an organization can also reduce the effects of losing out on an incredible hire, who could have been an indelible contribution to the company's future. As Farmer Pyne mentioned at the beginning of this chapter, if there is something that can personally be done to alleviate the issue of ghosting, it is in his best interest to explore and exercise every means to do so.

Candidates are not the only people who may ghost an organization. Employees may also "ghost" an employer, but in a more subtle manner, known as "quiet quitting."

Quiet Quitting

There is a catchphrase that seems to have received a lot of attention recently called "quiet quitting," made heavily popular by social media channels across the country. While ghosting is checking out without notice or explanation, quiet quitting is more of an apathetic approach to work, or "slacking off." It is not necessarily a new concept, though it seems to have inherited this new name as of late. It appears that, by giving it a new name, quiet quitting as a practice has now become acceptable or applauded.

The reality of such an approach by the employee is that it punishes the employer and even more so, the employee, even if they do not realize it. Quiet quitters will basically disengage at work, opting solely for minimal performance, instead of seeking high achievement in their efforts. The job conduct of such individuals is much like that of the gopher described in a previous chapter, gnawing away at the roots of the organization. Quiet quitters focus solely on their next paychecks. Sometimes they do not even engage with others. They just do the minimum to get through the day, and the thought of going above and beyond is not even entertained. Who is to blame in such a situation, and does giving only minimal effort seem the fair thing to do?

Quiet quitting worsens the employees' situations, so this type of behavior may be more detrimental to themselves than anyone else. First, it may cause the employees to hate their jobs even more than they already do. Often, they are frustrated with their tasks or the individuals they work with because there is a disconnect in communication, desire, and motivation. Due to the way the employees begin to act, the second problem is that they create negative reputations among their colleagues, who may become frustrated with their lack of effort and minimal output.

Finally, the employees are really wasting their time, talents, and potential career progress because they are just doing what is necessary to get by with an attitude of apathy. Since the employees are not happy, the best thing for them to do is to move on to something that better suits them and to not be afraid of such a transition.

There is no question that one of the results of the pandemic was a deeper awareness of burnout and dissatisfaction, leading to a brief "Great Resignation," as it has been called. People simply reevaluated their situations. These sentiments are still very fresh with the political turmoil, wars, rumors of wars, inflation, a possible recession on the horizon, and other factors that are still impacting the workforce in a variety of ways.

Ultimately, from the employer perspective, it is important to recognize some of the elements leading to ghosting, as previously mentioned in the chapter, since "quiet quitting" can come from similar apprehensions. Sometimes the worst thing an employer can do when they recognize the signs is to let it continue for an extended period of time. Ongoing conversations with the employees are the best ways to address the issue at hand, to determine whether there is an opportunity to mend the working relationship, or if it is better to part ways.

An employer may find that there are mental health factors that need some attention as well. Sometimes, quiet quitting is a call for help, due to depression or other mental health factors the employee may fail to comprehend or know how to address. This provides a unique opportunity for the employer to make a difference in the life of the employee. I have several friends who work in this field, and they would agree with me, that this "call for help" can sometimes be overlooked or misinterpreted.

In the job environment today, the biggest fear an employer has relating to letting someone go is the potential inability to replace the employee who is departing, possibly creating more work for the most valued employees, who are still dedicated to the organization. However, the principles outlined in this book should be a great starting point to diminish some of the fears when it comes to attracting and seeking out the replacement.

Farmer Pyne helped me recognize that, when it comes to ghosting and quiet quitting, there are some aspects that cannot be changed. However, if there are areas of the hiring process where employers can adjust and alleviate the ghosting issue, then it is in their best interest to do so.

A Shift in Mindset

For many candidates today, the job search is more than just finding a job. It's about finding meaning and purpose in what they do. It's about development and growth coupled with balance in all aspects of their lives. They need ongoing conversations and communication, not just the occasional review. They seek to find the answers to questions that will help them feel accomplished and fulfilled in their work.

Finally, they don't just want a boss. They want a coach who takes the time to lead. They want a mentor who takes the time to teach. They need an advocate who supports them in their work and celebrates their strengths and accomplishments. Mistakes are opportunities for growth, designed to teach lessons and increase their capacity for good. This is the mindset of workers today and in the future. When the job seekers cannot envision themselves in the role, or the employees cannot find purpose and meaning in what they do, they will simply disappear.

APPLE-LOGUE

PYNE FARMS has a dedicated spot on the farm that appears to be a big hill off the side of the road. As Farmer Pyne finished my first tour of his orchard all those years ago, we arrived at this smoldering pile of ash and branches. The smoke was still rising from the heap, and I could feel the warmth of the burning wood from trees that could no longer bear fruit worthy of picking.

As we approached, his boys were not only chucking dead branches into the fire, accompanied by roars of laughter and giggles, but they were also pulling up chairs nearby. Farmer Pyne reached into his tractor and pulled out bags of buns and hot dogs.

Much to the delight of everyone present, we all grabbed branches from the ground and filed the ends off just enough to slide a hot dog onto our makeshift roasting sticks. We then strategically placed them on a leaning teepee of sorts made from smaller branches, so that our food would slowly cook in the embers along the edges of the bonfire. Soon, bags of marshmallows, graham crackers, and bits of chocolate made their way to the feast, providing an incredible ending to the day, as the sun began to set in the west, blanketing the sky with streaks of pastel colors. The season itself had ended, and all the trees had been picked clean in preparation for the dormancy that awaited them during the winter months.

As I watched this scene unfold, I did not realize that this experience on the farm would lead to the creation of the Hiring Tree. My hope is that this book will inspire the reader to take a deeper dive into their own hiring process and to make the necessary changes to overcome the difficulties they face in attracting the right talent.

Kent and Steve: Springtime at Pyne Farms

Whether from the perspective of a business owner, a hiring manager involved in the process, or the recruiter and human resource professional assigned the task of filling roles within the organization, success will be achieved! I have seen thousands of companies apply these principles already, and the impact has been eye-opening and rewarding.

Like apple trees, these processes do not always bear fruit right away. One of my dearest friends at work, Heidi, reminded me the other day that a tree bears fruit in its season, and then, for the other seasons, it needs to be nourished and taken care of until it is time to bear fruit again. The advantage of establishing an organizational Hiring Tree is that the company *can* control the seasons.

For some industries, it is a constant drumbeat of growth and an increase of staff. For others, it is only an occasional need. Sometimes, it sneaks up unannounced, due to a resignation, accident, or other unforeseen circumstance. In all these scenarios, a steady and well-nourished Hiring Tree will have the ability to bear fruit when needed, as long as the company is willing to put in the work and dedication required, by continuing to nourish and strengthen it along the way. Patience and empathy will always be at the core of this process and will prove successful in both market types, where there is either a plethora of applicants or an applicant drought.

The wonderful news is that the fruit comes in both seasons when the Hiring Tree is properly cared for!

Endnotes

1 *Farm Show Magazine* – 1997 – Volume #21, Issue #3, Page 40.

2 Elliott Gold won an award in the 2021 Great American International Cider Competition held in New York City.

3 Joseph Smith is known as the founder of the Church of Jesus Christ of Latter-day Saints.

4 https://www.gallup.com/workplace/232955/no-employee-benefit-no-one-talking.aspx

5 As an example, a new law is going into effect in New York in Jan 2023. To learn more the reader is encouraged to research news articles on the subject: https://news.bloomberglaw.com/daily-labor-report/artificial-intelligence-hiring-bias-spurs-scrutiny-and-new-regs

6 *Washington: A Life* by Ron Chernow, Chapter 28, page 345.

7 SHRM, the Society for Human Resource Management, creates better workplaces where employers and employees thrive together. As the voice of all things work, workers and the workplace, SHRM is the foremost expert, convener and thought leader on issues impacting today's evolving workplaces. With 300,000+ HR and business executive members in 165 countries, SHRM impacts the lives of more than 115 million workers and families globally. https://www.shrm.org/about-shrm/Pages/default.aspx

8 Electronic Signature law requires the ability for the applicant to view or print what they have electronically signed, hence the need for the applicant to create an account. https://www.docusign.com/learn/esign-act-ueta

9 A disparate impact is when "policies, practices, rules or other systems that appear to be neutral result in a disproportionate impact on a protected group," as defined by the Society for Human Resource Management. https://www.shrm.org

10 Google is an American-based company that focuses on search engine technology.

11 Indeed is an American worldwide employment website for job listings.

12 An algorithm, in job search, is a set of instructions followed to calculate the best list of positions to display to the job seeker. It is like solving a problem following certain guidelines. The problem is that the job seeker wants to find a job, and the algorithm solves the problem by finding those roles that best fit the search parameters (rules or instructions) the job seeker has created.

13 Artificial intelligence is the simulation of human intelligence in machines that are programmed to think like humans and mimic their actions and problem-solving traits.

14 If the reader searches for "SEO keyword research," there are a variety of sources in this area that can be used.

15 Batteries Plus is a battery, lighting, smart home, key fob, and phone repair company that provides incredible solutions for both businesses and consumers alike. https://www.batteriesplus.com

16 https://www.utahshrm.org

17 There is a lot of debate as to the origin of this proverb, so I will leave it up to the reader to research and decide for themselves.

18 Jobs for America's Graduates (JAG) is a state-based, national non-profit organization dedicated to supporting young people who face significant challenges, to help them reach economic and academic success.

19 Tesla, Inc., is an American multinational automotive and clean energy company.

20 https://joinhandshake.com and https://www.symplicity.com respectively

21 https://www.linkedin.com/in/patrick-o-hara-83960252

22 https://www.inc.com/profile/applicantpro

23 https://newsroom.tiktok.com/en-us/find-a-job-with-tiktok-resumes

24 https://www.gallup.com/cliftonstrengths/en/350423/influential-good-manager.aspx

25 https://www.gallup.com/workplace/328121/disruption-reveals-engaging-millennial-employees.aspx

ACKNOWLEDGMENTS

I WANT TO EXPRESS MY GRATITUDE for those involved in the making of this book. First and foremost, I am grateful to Kent (Farmer Pyne), whose excitement and enthusiasm for his orchard led to the creation of the Hiring Tree analogy. A big thank you to Ryan and Heidi for their examples and inspiration that led to some great stories found within this book. I am grateful to Randy who reminded me that inspiration, no matter how trivial, comes from God, even in business endeavors. I am grateful to the cheer moms and volleyball moms who rooted me on while I researched and wrote during Ruby's and Katy's practices. A special thank you to Shannon Cave, my copy editor, who was willing to go above and beyond in her editing skills to help make the book more readable. Thank you to my mother, Frankie, for spending hours being my first reader and critic, and encouraging me to stay on schedule. Thank you to all of my colleagues and friends with SHRM and JAG who kept me on track and helped me stay accountable. Finally, thank you to my sweet wife, Alicia, who often fell asleep listening to me explain my ideas before putting them to paper.